SpringerBriefs in Economics

For further volumes:
http://www.springer.com/series/8876

Carol Yeh-Yun Lin · Leif Edvinsson
Jeffrey Chen · Tord Beding

National Intellectual Capital and the Financial Crisis in Argentina, Brazil, Chile, Colombia, Mexico, and Venezuela

Springer

Carol Yeh-Yun Lin
Department of Business Administration
National Chengchi University
Taipei
Taiwan

Leif Edvinsson
Universal Networking Intellectual Capital
Norrtälje
Sweden

Jeffrey Chen
Accenture
Chicago, IL
USA

Tord Beding
TC-Growth AB
Karlstad
Sweden

ISSN 2191-5504 ISSN 2191-5512 (electronic)
ISBN 978-1-4614-8920-7 ISBN 978-1-4614-8921-4 (eBook)
DOI 10.1007/978-1-4614-8921-4
Springer New York Heidelberg Dordrecht London

Library of Congress Control Number: 2013946941

Printed on acid-free paper

Springer is part of Springer Science+Business Media (www.springer.com)

Foreword I

The economic crisis is a consequence of many parallel factors which are all related to globalization and digitalization. My main concern, assessing this in more detail from the European perspective, is that revolutionary global forces have not been taken early nor seriously enough by most national and regional decision-makers. The Heads of European States and Governments have once again recalled the importance of fiscal consolidation, structural reform, and targeted investment to put Europe back on the path of smart, sustainable, and inclusive growth. The main question is how capable and ready are the national governments to tackling the complex and manifold issues of crises and to renewing even radically many of our public and private structures and processes.

The first basic requirement is that all the European Union Member States remain fully committed to taking the actions required at the national level to achieve the objectives of the Europe 2020 Strategy. The second basic requirement is that the national and regional governments, as well as people, are ready for radical changes. This booklet, and the other 11 booklets by experienced authors, focus on national intellectual capital and give necessary insights and facts for us the readers and especially for our in-depth systemic thinking of the interrelationships of NIC and economic recovery.

How should the national and regional decision-makers tackle the existing knowledge of intangible capital? The focus needs to be more on the bottom-up approach stressing the developments at local and regional levels. I highlight our recent statements by the EU Committee of Regions. The key priorities are to get more innovations out of research and to encourage mindset change toward open innovation.

The political decision-makers are finally aware that the traditional indicators created for and used in industrial production cannot be applied to a knowledge-intensive, turbulent, and innovativeness-based global enterprise environment. Indicators that perceive the intangible dimensions of competitiveness—knowledge capital, innovation knowledge, and anticipation of the future—have been developed around the world, but their use has not yet become established in practice. This booklet accelerates the development and use of these indicators.

This helps the local and regional, as well as central, governments in taking brave leaps forward on a practical level—giving greater ownership and involving all the stakeholders. This means the need of actions towards increasing the structural and relational capital of regions, both internally in communities of practice and in collaboration with others.

The new generation innovation activities are socially motivated, open, and collectively participated, complex and global by nature. The regions need to move towards open innovation, within a human-centered vision of partnerships between public and private sector actors, with universities playing a crucial role.

Regions should be encouraged to develop regional innovation platforms, which act as demand-based service centres and promote the use of international knowledge to implement the Europe 2020 Strategy, smart specialization and European partnerships according to the interests and needs of regions. For this to happen, we need to apply the new dynamic understanding of regional innovation ecosystems, in which companies, cities, and universities as well as other public and private sector actors (the "Triple Helix") learn to work together in new and creative ways to fully harness their innovative potential.

New innovative practices do not come about by themselves. One major potential is the use of public procurement. The renewing of the European wide rules must increase the strategic agility and activities of municipalities and other public operators as creators of new solutions. Especially, the execution of pre-commercial procurement should be reinforced even more in combination with open innovation to speed-up the green knowledge society development, i.e., for common re-usable solutions in creating the infrastructures and services modern real-world innovation ecosystems are built upon. Conditions must be created that also allow for extensive development projects which address complex societal challenges and which take the form of risk-taking consortia.

One of our working instruments within the Committee of the Regions is the Europe 2020 Monitoring Platform, which broadly reviews and reflects the opinions and decisions on regional level all around Europe. It gives a flavor of cultural and other socioeconomic differences inside the EU. This brings an important perspective to the intellectual capital, namely the values and attitudes needed for citizens supporting policymakers on appropriate long-term investments and policies.

Emphasizing the importance of these issues, decision makers in all countries and regions worldwide need a deep and broad understanding of the critical success factors affecting the NIC. With all the facts and frames for thinking this booklet gives a valuable insight in today's challenges.

Markku Markkula
Advisor to the Aalto University Presidents
Member of the EU Committee of the Regions
Former Member of the Parliament of Finland

Foreword II

Financial crisis—words very much heard today. What is all this about, actually, and how to get a grip on what we experience today? The booklet gives an important insight into the factors affecting competitiveness and productivity in modern knowledge society. We need to see behind the obvious, and we need to have increasingly "qualified guesses" as the character of the society and industry has fundamentally changed.

What is very important to notice is the shift toward intangible value creation beyond the deterministic phenomena we saw very clearly in the industrial era. Cost drivers were the important ones throughout the industry. Mass production, bigger is better; very traditional productivity factors, was the mantra.

However, the production picture is changing. Increasingly, value is created by the intangibles, often services related to the tangible components, and even totally in immaterial value creation, where perceptions and expectations determine the market value of the "extended product." We also see rapid change in organizational forms, we see new type of entrepreneurship growing besides the traditional industry clusters, we see smart specialization of regions and countries.

This means also that there will be clearly different and complementary roles of the actors in innovation and value creation ecosystems. Large companies, small ones and even microenterprises together with the public sector are traditionally seen as the active partners in such innovation environments. The real issue in the dynamic markets is however that the end users are increasingly to be taken on board as *active subjects* for innovation, and not merely treated as objects, customers. Markets need to be shaped and created in a much more dynamic way than ever before. Open innovation beyond cross-licensing includes the societal capital as an important intangible engine for productivity growth. Innovation happens only when the offering is meeting the demand. Otherwise we can only speak about inventions or ideas.

We need to have a close look at the intellectual capital and the different factors within it when we design our policy approaches. Short-term investments in process capital (infrastructures) and market capital seem to be very important for the manufacturing base as such, but at the same time measures for longer term intellectual capital development and efficiency need to be taken.

Increasingly, important is the *structure* and the open *processes* related to intangible capital and knowledge pools. For sustainable long-term development both the *human capital and renewal capital are crucial*, as they are directly related to the innovation capability of the region. The correlation between these factors and the GDP growth is undisputable. In knowledge intense industries talent is attracting talent, and the connectivity which modern ICT provides makes this talent pool fluid across disciplines, organizations, and geographical settings. It is imperative to modernize the innovation systems enabling the full dynamics needed for success in knowledge intense industries, beyond the traditional boundaries.

Measuring performance of innovation systems becomes increasingly complex due to the mash-up of different disciplines, having new types of actors and interactions between them. Hence, the importance of analysis of the various components of the national intellectual capital (NIC) (and equally on national innovation capability) as done in this booklet cannot be underestimated when making qualified guesses for operational choices to create functioning innovation ecosystems. The only predictable in true innovation is the unpredictability and the surprises. The role of the public sector is to drive strategy and measures enabling the unpredictable, and to catalyze a fluid, seamless, and frictionless innovation system to grow, with strong interplay with the surrounding society.

We need to have the courage to experiment, to prototype in real-world settings, to have all stakeholders involved to find and remove the friction points of innovation, and to achieve sustainable innovation ecosystems for knowledge intense products and services.

I wish you interesting reading with this mind opening report.

Bror Salmelin
Advisor, Innovation Systems
European Commission
DG CONNECT

Foreword III

The 2008 global financial crisis hit the whole world with unprecedented speed, causing widespread financial panic. Consumer confidence dropped to the lowest level since the Great Depression. Taiwan, with an export-dependent economy, was seriously impacted by the crisis and the unemployment rate hiked while household consumption levels dropped. At the onset of the financial crisis, Prof. Lin was the Dean of Student Affairs here at National Chengchi University in Taipei, Taiwan. She was the dean in charge of financial aid and student loans and thus saw firsthand the direct impact the financial crisis had upon our students. The crisis was so devastating that Prof. Lin, along with the university, was compelled to launch several new initiatives to raise money and help students weather the difficult times.

I am very glad that she took this painful experience to heart and set herself upon the task of investigating the impact of the crisis; trying to look into the causes and consequences for policy implications, not only for Taiwan but for an array of 48 countries. In particular, she approaches the crisis from the perspective of "National Intellectual Capital, (NIC)" which is very important in today's knowledge-driven economy.

Taiwan is an example of a knowledge economy and has enjoyed the fame of being referred to as a "high-tech island". Without an abundance of natural resources, Taiwan's hardworking and highly educated population is the single most precious resource that the island has. Acknowledging the value of such human resources and intellectual capital, we established the Taiwan Intellectual Capital Research Center (TICRC) under my leadership in 2003. Ever since then, Taiwan's government has continuously funded the university to conduct relevant research projects aimed at enhancing the intellectual capital of Taiwan. Having been thus endowed with the responsibility of nourishing future leaders in the public and private sectors, we have focused on building up our strength in innovation, entrepreneurship, and technology management-related research and education.

To enhance intellectual capital research, we recently formed a joint team of professors for a 4-year project in order to leverage their respective research capabilities. Through this project we hope to provide policy suggestions for the government by exploring the creativity, innovation, and intellectual capital at national, regional, city, and county levels. The goal is to come up with an intangible assets (IA) agenda for Taiwan's future sustainability. Prof. Lin is an integral member in this research team.

Following her 2011 book *National Intellectual Capital: A Comparison of 40 Countries*, this booklet series is Prof. Lin's second attempt at presenting her research, conducted under the sponsorship of TICRC, to international readers. As the Founding Director of TICRC and her President, I am honored to give a brief introduction of the value of this booklet series.

In comparison to her 2011 book, this series increased the number of countries studied to 48 and particularly focuses on the impact of intellectual capital on the 2008 global financial crisis. Rarely has an economic issue been systematically studied from the view point of IA, particularly at such a large scale of 48 countries. The research results show without a doubt that NIC is indeed an important economic development enhancer. In particular, the fact that countries with higher NIC experienced faster recoveries from the 2008 financial crisis provides a strong message for the policymakers.

In addition to providing insights to national policy, the booklet also summarizes the background of each country before the crisis, the key events during the crisis, economic development afterwards, and future prospects and challenges. Each volume affords readers a holistic picture of what happened in each country in an efficient manner. The linkage between NIC and this financial crisis also provides a different perspective of the crisis.

We are happy that Prof. Lin continues to share her valuable research results with international readers. I sincerely hope that her insights can garner more attention concerning the benefits of developing NIC for the well-being of every nation.

Se-Hwa Wu
Professor, Graduate Institute of Technology
and Innovation Management
President, National Chengchi University
Taipei, Taiwan

Preface I

There are "mounting risks of a breakup of the Euro zone." Such comments are frequent today on how the European leaders are handling the escalating crisis and its potential impact on non-European countries. But few leaders, reporters, or researchers are actually addressing the situation of National Intellectual Capital (NIC) and its signals. In addition to the financial crisis, is there an emerging NIC crisis as well? Why is it emerging? How should policymakers think about NIC? In what way does it need specific attention? When will the outcome and impact of taken NIC policy steps be realized?

In the midst of the European crisis, there are national interventions to address the issues mentioned above. In leading economical nations the investments going into intangibles now exceeds tangibles, and is positively correlated to income per capita. However, these still do not show up clearly in national mapping as well as policy making insights. Therefore the New Club of Paris is focusing the knowledge agenda setting for countries on Societal Innovation (see www.new-club-of-paris.org).

Chairman Ben Bernanke of the U.S. Federal Reserve was addressing some of these same aspects in a key note speech in May 2011 hosted by Georgetown University: http://www.icapitaladvisors.com/2011/05/31/bernanke-on-intangible-capital/. OECD and the World Bank are developing NIC statistics, often based on the model from Corrado–Hultén. Japan has been developing both NIC and Intangible Assets (IA) at METI for some time now. Their research on IC/IA has resulted in a National IA Week with various key stakeholders, such as government agencies, universities, stock exchange, and enterprises. Japan is so far the only country in the world to hold such activities, and they have been doing so for the last 8 years. Australia, Singapore, South Korea, and China are currently undertaking various NIC initiatives. Other countries are also becoming more and more aware of NIC, with policy rhetoric centered on innovation, education, R&D, and trade. Despite this, the map for a more justified NIC navigation has been missing.

This booklet highlights NIC development for a number of countries, based on 48 different indicators, aggregated into four major NIC components of human capital, market capital, process capital, and renewal capital. The model here is a refined and verified statistical model in comparison to the Corrado–Hultén model. We call it the L–E–S model after the contributors Lin–Edvinsson–Stahle. Based on a deeper understanding and the timeline pattern it sets forth, this model will add to a better NIC navigation, not to mention knowledge agenda setting for countries.

Upon looking at a global cluster NIC map, it is evident that the top leading countries seem to be small countries, especially Singapore, the Nordic countries, Hong Kong, and Taiwan. For the U.S., Finland, and Sweden around 50 % or more of its economical growth is related to NIC aspects. Sweden, Finland, Switzerland, the U.S., Israel, and Denmark are strongly influenced in its GDP growth by focusing on Renewal Capital.

It might be that we will see a clearer map of the NIC ecosystem and drivers for wealth emerge in the extension of this ongoing unique research of NIC. This booklet will present a NIC map for various clusters of countries. It can be used for bench marking as well as bench learning for policy prototyping. The starting point is awareness and thinking of NIC, and its drivers for economic results. Based on this more refined navigation, NIC metrics can be presented.

Deeper understanding will emerge from this research, such as the scaling up of limited skilled human capital in one nation by using the globalized broadband technologies for migration and flow of knowledge (such as tele-medicine or mobile banking in Africa). This is also referred to as the IC multiplier. It might also be the way the old British Commonwealth was constructed, but without the IC taxonomy. In modern taxonomy it might be the shaping of NIC alliances for the migration and flow of IC between nations?

Another understanding that might emerge for policy making is the issue of employment versus unemployment. The critical understanding will be deployment of IC drivers. This will require another networked workforce of value networkers on a global scale, such as volunteering software and apps developers. However such volunteers do not show up in traditional statistics, for the mapping on behalf of policymakers.

On another level, there might be a clear gap analyses between nations to support the vision process of a nation. On a deeper level, it is also a leadership responsibility to address the gap of NIC positions versus potential positions. Such a gap is in fact a liability to the citizens, to be addressed in due time.

This will take us to the need for the continuous renewal of social systems. The so-called Arab Spring is explained by some as resulting from three drivers: lack of renewal of social systems, Internet, and soccer as cross-class interaction space. The lack of social renewal and innovation is most likely critical early warning signals. For Greece, we can see such a tipping point occurred back in 1999.

On a global scale we might see that the concern for the Euro zone crisis should and can be explained by a deeper and supplementary understanding of NIC, in addition to financial capital. So we need to refine our NIC understanding, NIC mapping, NIC metrics, and NIC organizational constructs into societal innovation for the benefit of wealth creation of subsequent generations.

Leif Edvinsson
The World's First Professor of Intellectual Capital
Chairman and Co-founder of New Club of Paris

Preface II

Our first book *National Intellectual Capital: A Comparison of 40 Countries* was published in early 2011, at a time when the 2008 global financial crisis had been declared over yet the European region was still plagued with sovereign debt problems. Before we finalized the book, we were able to retrieve some of our raw data concerning the troubled countries, such as Greece, Iceland, Ireland, Portugal, and Spain. The results of our analysis based on data spanning 1995–2008 revealed some early warning signs of the financial turmoil in those countries. In my preface of that book, I mentioned the warning signs might reveal only the tip of an iceberg. At that time, my co-author, Prof. Edvinsson and I decided to do a follow-up study to trace the development of National Intellectual Capital (NIC) in as many countries as possible, particularly through the lens of the 2008 global financial crisis. This 12-booklet series is the result of that determination.

The 2008 global financial crisis came with unexpected speed and had such a wide-spread effect that surprised many countries far from the epicenter of the initial U.S. sub-prime financial problem, geographically and financially. According to reports, no country was immune from the impact of this financial crisis. Such development clearly signifies how closely connected the world has become and the importance of having a global interdependent view. By reporting what happened during 2005–2010 in 48 major countries throughout the world, this booklet series serves the purpose of uncovering national problems before the crisis, government coping strategies, stimulus plans, potential prospects, and challenges of each individual country, and the interdependence between countries. The 6 years of data allow us to compare NIC and economic development crossing before, during, and after the financial crisis. They are handy booklets for readers to have a quick yet overall view of countries of personal interest. The list of 48 countries in 11 clusters is provided in the appendix of each booklet.

Searching for financial crisis-related literature for 48 countries is itself a very daunting task, not to mention summarizing and analyzing it. For financial crisis-related literature, we mainly relied on the reports and statistics of certain world organizations, including OECD, World Bank, United Nations, International Monetary Fund (IMF), European Commission Office, the US Congressional Research Service, the U.S. Central Intelligence Agency, and International Labor Office (ILO). Some reliable research centers, such as the National Bureau of

Economic Research in the U.S., World Economic Forum, the Heritage Foundation in the U.S., and government websites from each country were also our sources of information. Due to the requirement of more update and comprehensive information, we were not able to use as much academic literature as we would have liked, because it generally covers a very specific topic with time lag and with research methods not easily comprehended by the general public. Therefore, we had to resort to some online news reports for more current information.

In the middle of 2012, the lasting financial troubles caused the European economy to tilt back into a recession, which also slowed down economic growth across the globe. However, almost 4 years have passed since the outbreak of the global financial crisis in late 2008; it is about time to reflect on what happened and the impact of the financial crisis. By comparing so many countries, we came to a preliminary conclusion that countries with faster recovery from the financial crisis have higher NIC than those with slower recovery. In other words, countries that rebounded fast from the crisis generally have solid NIC fundamentals, including human capital, market capital, process capital, and renewal capital. We also found that the higher the NIC, the higher the GDP per capita (ppp). This booklet series provides a different perspective to look beyond the traditional economic indicators for national development.

In an era when IA have become a key competitive advantage, investing in NIC development is investing in future national development and well-being.

Enjoy!

Carol Yeh-Yun Lin
Professor, Department of Business Administration
National Chengchi University, Taiwan
Taiwan Intellectual Capital Research Center (TICRC)

Executive Summary

National Intellectual Capital keeps non-oil export countries competitive, as in thecase of Chile.

How can National Intellectual Capital (NIC) act as a policy guideline for national well-being? One of the key causes of the financial crisis was that conventional financial systems failed to detect potential risks due to non-transparent information disclosure, including unsupervised financial activities across national borders. Our earlier NIC research revealed warning signs of impending financial crisis for Greece and Ireland. Such findings indicate that NIC, albeit intangible, can provide valuable insights into risk control and strategy formulation. This booklet looks at the connections between the financial crisis and NIC development for Argentina, Brazil, Chile, Colombia, Mexico, and Venezuela.

In particular, this report attempts to answer the following questions: How did these countries weather the financial crisis? Why are the oil-rich and national resource rich Latin American countries still in great poverty? What are the NIC profiles of these countries? What role has NIC played in the national development of these countries? Why has Chile, as a non-oil-dependent country, developed better than the oil-rich countries in this region?

Data covering 2005–2010 for 48 countries indicate that *the higher the NIC, the higher the GDP per capita (ppp)*, accentuating the value of NIC as a driver in major countries throughout the world. *For the 6-year average of NIC rankings among 48 countries, Argentina ranks 45th, Brazil 42nd, Chile 30th, Colombia 41st, Mexico 43rd, and Venezuela 48th.* In general, these countries are in the last quartile of 48-country NIC, except Chile.

The 2008 financial crisis caused severe impacts across the globe and is considered to be the worst crisis since the Great Depression of the 1930s. The crisis came with unexpected speed and spread into a global economic shock, which resulted in a number of bank failures. During this period, economies worldwide slowed, credits tightened, and international trade declined. In an effort to mitigate the crisis, governments and central banks across the globe responded with unprecedented fiscal stimuli, monetary policy expansions, and institutional bailouts. These measures had its desired impact and the financial crisis was declared over by the end of 2009.

However, the short global recovery in 2010 was overshadowed by the lingering sovereign debt problems in Europe, thus a global economic slowdown recurred in the second half of 2011. Despite the efforts of European leaders to prevent large economies like Italy and Spain from needing bailouts, Spain still asked for external financial assistance in June of 2012. Although the global economic outlook for 2013 will be better than that of 2012, growth in most developed countries is still predicted to be weak.

During the financial crisis, these six Latin American countries were relatively resilient compared to other countries for the following reasons:

First, past crises in the last few decades have prompted these countries to tighten financial regulations and launched structural reforms.

Second, foreign direct investment capital flight was not serious as this region was not yet the most favorable investing place.

Third, abundant international reserves of oil-rich countries plus price increases in oil and commodities allowed most of these countries to have some leeway in dealing with the crisis. In general, relatively sound macroeconomic fundamentals, policy responses by the governments, and international financial support have ameliorated what could have been a deeper and longer regional decline.

The Global Competitiveness Index ranking (GCI, Fig. 1.1) of these countries (except Brazil) declined in 2011–2012, when compared to their 2005–2006 level. Argentina declined from 72 to 85, Chile from 23 to 31, Colombia from 57 to 68, Mexico from 55 to 58, and Venezuela from 89 to 124. Only Brazil advanced in GCI, from 65 to 53. Between 2005 and 2010, the real *GDP growth* pattern of these countries (except Venezuela) was largely similar—it leveled in 2008, dropped to negative growth in 2009, and then rebounded to positive growth in 2010. However, Mexico experienced an earlier GDP growth decline from 2007 and had the deepest drop in 2009. Venezuela was the only country that did not rebound to positive GDP growth (−2.89 %) in 2010. Venezuela also has the lowest NIC ranking out of any country, 48 out of 48.

In terms of general *government debt*, only Chile and Mexico increased their debt level in 2010 compared to 2005. However, Chile had exceptionally low government debt even in 2010 at only 9.19 % of its GDP. Mexico had government debt of 42.70 % in 2010, still lower than the EU criteria of 60 % GDP. Argentina was able to reduce its government debt to a very large scale, from 85.42 % in 2005 to 47.09 % in 2010, very likely due to a global rise in soy bean prices. In 2010, Brazil had the highest government debt level in this country group, reaching 54.74 % GDP.

Aside from GDP growth and government debt, *unemployment* and its social impact is one of the major concerns of the financial crisis. Except for Mexico, all the other countries had unemployment rate reduction in 2010, compared to 2005. Argentina had the most significant reduction from 11.50 % in 2005 to 7.40 % in 2010, followed by Brazil from 9.80 to 6.70 %, and Venezuela from 8.90 to 6.50 %. Consistently, Colombia had the highest and Mexico the lowest unemployment rate over the years, the former 11.80 % and the latter 5.40 % in 2010. With respect to *Consumer Price Inflation* (*CPI*), Venezuela consistently had the highest and

Argentina the second highest CPI reaching 27.20 % and 10.57 % in 2010, respectively. Chile had the lowest CPI, which dropped to 1.41 % only in 2010. The CPI of the other three countries was very close to each other, ranging from 3 to 6 %, with flat development over the 6 years.

For NIC component capitals, over the studied 6 years (2005–2010), Human Capital (HC) did not vary much among these countries before 2008. From 2009, two clusters appeared with Argentina and Chile being the high HC group and the rest four countries the low group. In general, the HC of these six countries was in the last quarter amongst the 48 countries, ranking between 35 and 44. Particularly, their "higher education enrollment" scored very low, ranging from 1.51 to 3.5 on 1–10 scale. Market Capital (MC) scores were spreading, with Chile far ahead of the others; Brazil, Colombia, and Mexico comprised a middle group, and Argentina and Venezuela a low group. For Process Capital (PC), Chile consistently had the highest, Colombia the second highest, and Venezuela the lowest in the group. The other three countries were in the middle.

For Renewal Capital (RC), all the six countries were very low, ranging from 1.2 to 1.8 on a scale of 1–10. Financial capital (based on 1–10 scale) did not show much difference among these six countries. For the overall NIC, Chile consistently had the highest score and Venezuela the lowest, with the other four countries in-between with little score variation, especially in the most recent 2009 and 2010.

For the co-development of NIC-GDP, MC-GDP, and PC-GDP, Chile performed best, whereas Venezuela performed worst. In terms of long-term NIC (HC+RC), Chile was the best performer and Mexico and Venezuela the lowest performer. As for short-term NIC (MC+PC), Chile again outdid the other countries, with Venezuela coming in last.

For *dynamic NIC ranking* changes in three time periods (2005–2006, 2007–2008, 2009–2010), the ranking gains represent increasing international competitiveness (among the 48 countries) after the financial crisis. Argentina gained international competitiveness after the financial crisis in HC, FC, and overall NIC. Brazil gained the largest scale of international competitiveness in MC and RC after the crisis, although it lost one rank each in HC and PC, comparing the most recent period (2009–2010) with 6 years average ranking. Chile lost three ranks of RC comparing the same time periods, which is a warning for this best performer in the group. Colombia lost one rank to two ranks in HC, PC, RC, and overall NIC also comparing the same time periods. Mexico lost two to three ranks in MC, FC, and overall NIC comparing the same time periods. Venezuela did not have much ranking changes over the three time periods.

NIC *3D trajectory analysis* was conducted to detect the enhancing and impeding factors of each country in reaching a targeted GDP per capita (ppp), benchmarking Germany due to its best performance in the Euro area. To reach the GDP level of Germany, Venezuela has the longest distance (−83.29 %) to cover, followed by Argentina (−69.30 %), Colombia (−66.56 %), Mexico (−63.94 %), Brazil (−62.72 %), and Chile (−57.56 %). Interestingly, even though Argentina weathered this financial crisis better than Colombia, it still had a longer route to reach the target. A likely answer is that Colombia had better MC and PC than Argentina, despite Colombia experiencing more ranking declines during the three time periods. Specifically, transparency of government policies, capital availability, and convenience of establishing new firms are much better in Colombia than Argentina. However, it can be anticipated that Argentina will catch up with Colombia pretty soon, if the latter stands still without further progress for the next few years.

As of early 2013, the world economic recovery has been hampered by the pending debt problems in the Euro zone, the modest growth in the U.S., and the slower growth in Asia. Although these Latin American countries showed their resilience during this financial crisis, challenges still lie ahead as described in Chap. 5.

The 2008 global financial crisis provided an ideal opportunity for nations to examine/renew/innovate the soundness of their economic system and the effectiveness of *national governance related to NIC*. The following implications are drawn from our research findings. Readers can refer to Chap. 5 for the rationale behind these implications.

1. NIC development goes together with the economic development and should be regarded as an enhancer of economic growth.
2. Latin American countries can utilize their relatively good short-term NIC—MC and PC to boost national development.
3. NIC keeps non-oil export countries competitive, as in the case of Chile.
4. Positive NIC ranking changes reflect national competiveness.
5. Government-related issues constitute a major part of impeding factors in achieving GDP growth in this region.
6. Research and development investment should lead to further national development in this region.
7. Oil and commodity-dependent countries need NIC to facilitate national development and establish better governance systems for a more resilient economy free from the risk of external shock.
8. Argentina's good performance during this global financial crisis may pave the way for its future development.

This report uncovers that Argentina needs to pay more attention to its high inflation and capital flight problems. Although rapidly expanding, Brazil needs to attend to its social and environmental problems as well. Chile, being the best performer in this group tangibly and intangibly, needs to have a coping strategy with respect to its low and declining RC. Colombia, an oil-rich country, can utilize its wealth to upgrade the infrastructure and reduce poverty and inequality. Its declining NIC also sent a warning for the sustainability of the country. Mexico needs to seriously deal with its chronic educational problem and informal economic system. For further progress, its oil technology has to be advanced as well. Contrary to expectation, this oil export country had a relatively large-scale MC decline over the 6 years. Venezuela's lowest NIC ranking reveals critical societal problems that need to be dealt with. Despite its wealth, Venezuela still performed poorly during and after this financial crisis. First and foremost, its financial system needs to be re-examined for future sustainability.

In an era when the intangible asset has become a key competitive advantage, investing in NIC development is in essence investing in future national development and well-being. NIC should be nourished from both local culture viewpoint and global interconnectivity by social media. Based on emerging new insights of values, societal history, and citizen relationships, a key focus for the future will be on the fusion of NIC and social service innovation as well as societal innovation, for the enabling of a new societal fabric.

Contents

List of Figures

List of Tables

Appendices

Abstract

In the first decade of the new millennium, the biggest event that caught worldwide attention was the 2008 global financial crisis, which was brought about primarily by ineffective governance, failed surveillance systems, and implementation flaws. These problems are mainly intangible in nature. Therefore, examining the financial crisis from the viewpoint of intangible asset provides a different perspective from traditional economic approaches. National intellectual capital (NIC), mainly consisting of human capital, market capital, process capital, renewal capital, and financial capital is a valuable intangible asset and a key source of national competitive advantage and well-being in today's knowledge economy. This booklet looks into the connections between the 2008 global financial crisis and NIC development with a special focus on Argentina, Brazil, Chile, Colombia, Mexico, and Venezuela. In addition to the summaries of financial crisis impact, the aftermath, future prospects, and challenges of each individual country, NIC analysis based on data covering 2005–2010 for 48 countries reveal that the higher the NIC, the higher the GDP per capita (ppp). Graphical presentations of various types allow for intra-country and inter-country comparisons to position the reported six countries on a world map of NIC-GDP co-development. By looking into tangible economic development along with intangible NIC development, this booklet provides valuable implications for policymakers.

Keywords Competitiveness · Economic policy · Financial capital · Human capital · Innovation · Intangible assets · Intellectual capital · Knowledge management · Research and development (R&D) · Science and technology policy ·

Chapter 1
Introduction

In early 2013, the International Monetary Fund (2013) projected that global growth will increase during 2013 as policy actions have lowered acute crisis risks in the Euro area and the United States. However, the recovery in the Euro area was slower than expected, Japan has slid into recession, and there are risks of excessive near-term fiscal consolidation in the United States. Nevertheless, policies have supported a modest growth pickup in some emerging market economies and global growth could be stronger if financial conditions continue to improve.

In 2012, the U.S. economy was growing but performance remained below what was expected and a slowdown surfaced in many emerging economies, partly reflecting the impact of the recession in Europe (Elliott 2012). In China, India and Brazil, production growth also slowed due to a reduction in export and lower domestic spending (CPB 2012). In hindsight, it is valuable to reflect upon what happened during the past few years to gain some insights for future preventive actions.

The 2008 global financial crisis is considered by many economists to be the worst one since the Great Depression of the 1930s. The crisis rapidly developed and spread into a global economic shock, which resulted in a number of European bank failures (Altman 2009; Fackler 2008). World political leaders, national ministers of finance, and central bank directors coordinated their efforts to reduce fear, but the crisis continued and eventually led to a global currency crisis. During this period, economies worldwide slowed, credits tightened, and international trade declined.

After the full force of the financial crisis hit in October 2008, there was a call in the United States for a hands-off policy in order to let the markets "work themselves out", in accordance with how capitalism was theoretically supposed to work. Yet, the U.S. Federal Reserve Chairman Ben Bernanke believed that such a policy would be catastrophic and urged government intervention. In a statement to Congress, Mr. Bernanke said, "If we let the banking system fail, no one will talk about the Great Depression anymore, because this will be so much worse" (Reavis 2009). As a result, the U.S. government decided to take action to prevent such a failure.

C. Y.-Y. Lin et al., *National Intellectual Capital and the Financial Crisis in Argentina, Brazil, Chile, Colombia, Mexico, and Venezuela*, SpringerBriefs in Economics,
DOI: 10.1007/978-1-4614-8921-4_1,

Following the lead of the United States, governments and central banks worldwide responded to the international crisis with unprecedented fiscal stimuli, monetary policy expansions and institutional bailouts in their respective countries. The financial rescue worked and an economic crisis akin to The Great Depression was avoided. In fact, the crisis was declared over by the third quarter of 2009 (Kehoe 2010). While the crisis was officially over, economic recovery in most developed countries continued to trudge along beneath prerecession levels (Norris 2011).

During the early stages of the financial crisis, management scholars criticized the inability of traditional accounting systems to reveal the intangibles that explain hidden risks as well as values for proper decision making (Reavis 2009). In line with the importance of the intangibles, advocating the value of intellectual capital, human capital, social capital, and the like has gained increasing attention in today's keener global competition (Edvinsson and Malone 1997).

It is our deep belief that national intellectual capital, albeit intangible, can provide valuable insights to policy makers regarding future risk control and strategy formulation. Our previous book, *National Intellectual Capital: A Comparison of 40 Countries* (Lin and Edvinsson 2011; www.nic40.org), was born out of this belief and traces the national intellectual capital development of 40 countries over a 14-year period from 1995 to 2008. The data analysis presented in our previous work revealed certain early warning signs of impending financial crisis for countries such as Greece and Ireland (Lin and Edvinsson 2011, pp. 327–333). As a follow-up study, this booklet series is an attempt to further understand the connections between the 2008 global financial crisis and national intellectual capital (NIC) development.

The booklet series, in its entirety, will examine the NIC statuses of 48 countries from the period of 2005–2010 to glean new understanding about whether there is a NIC development pattern that distinguishes fast recovery countries from slow recovery ones. This is presented through a series of 11 country clusters, with one booklet focusing on one particular cluster. The clusters are determined based on several factors: geographical proximity, similar size, or similar phase of economic development. Focusing on one cluster at a time, we first probe the issues of concern within a single country, then extend to compare multiple countries to see whether the situation before and after the crisis can be explained by the intangible NIC. Our data comes from the well-recognized International Institute for Management Development (IMD) in Switzerland. The IMD has been publishing yearly rankings of World Competitiveness for around two decades. Hopefully, the analysis in this booklet series can provide a different perspective of the financial crisis for future policy implications.

This volume, Volume Nine, will focus on the six Latin American countries of Argentina, Brazil, Chile, Colombia, Mexico, and Venezuela as they have language and culture similarities as well as geographical proximity that make it easy to compare and examine them as a cluster. This booklet first provides an economic background to these six countries as a whole before going into each individual country's development. Through this process, the authors hope to paint a general picture of the economic condition and provide a basis for our dataset and analysis in future sections.

Chapter 2 briefly introduces the impact of 2008 financial crisis on the six countries. Chapter 3 discusses the NIC development of these countries. Chapter 4 describes issues beyond the financial crisis and Chap. 5 concludes with future perspective and policy implications.

Economic Background

Since the economic history of these six countries goes back centuries, it is impossible to cover the entire spectrum in this work. As such, this background discussion will consider events in the relative recent history from 2005 onwards that have the most direct impact upon the current economic conditions of each specific country. In addition, particular attention will be given to the 2008 global financial crisis. In doing so, the authors hope that the background, in conjunction with our later data and analysis, will provide a "before, during, and after" picture of what was happening from a macroeconomic and intangible assets viewpoint.

To paint a general picture about their global competitiveness in the most recent years and before the financial crisis, we introduce hereunder the Global Competitiveness Index (GCI) published by the World Economic Forum for readers' reference. This index is relatively robust, as it takes into account the 12 distinct pillars[1] containing basic requirements, efficiency enhancers, and innovation factors that contribute to a nation's overall economic strength. Based upon commonly accepted economic theory, the development of a total 142 countries was split into three stages in which different factors play the dominant role in determining the outcome of a country's economy. Stage 1, Stage 2, and Stage 3 are respectively characterized by being factor, efficiency, and innovation-driven (Schwab 2011).

Taking each country's annual ranking and plotting against a time series of seven periods, Fig. 1.1 displays a rough pictorial overview of the six countries' global competitiveness changes before and after the financial crisis. From the figure, it can be seen that over the past seven years, the competitiveness ranking of the six countries has been relatively stable, except for Venezuela taking a more apparent downturn from 89 to 124. Argentina and Colombia also lost global competitiveness by declining 13 and 11 ranks (85–72 and 68–57), respectively, over the seven-year period. However in the last period, Argentina, Brazil, and Mexico gained global competitiveness with ranking advancement, whereas Colombia remained at the same ranking and Chile declined one rank when

[1] The 12 pillars include: institutions, infrastructure, macroeconomic environment, health and primary education, higher education and training, goods market efficiency, labor market efficiency, financial market development, technological readiness, market size, business sophistication, and innovation.

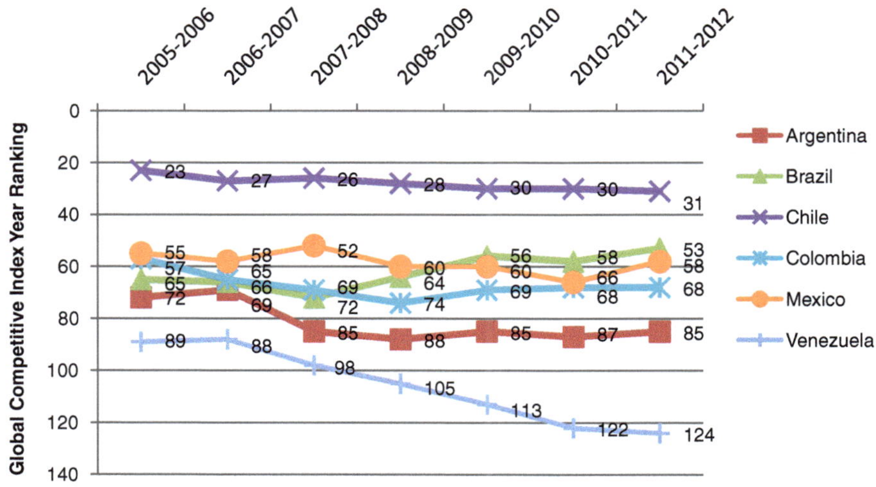

Fig. 1.1 GCI ranking of the six Latin American countries

compared to the previous period. In general, this trend reflects the recovery from the financial crisis in these countries except Venezuela.

One 2012 study conducted by OECD and the United Nations (2012) also showed good recovery of the major Latin America countries as presented in Fig. 1.1. With the gradual consolidation and strengthening of democratic systems, most of Latin American countries resisted the economic and financial crisis well, mainly due to their responsible macroeconomic management and structural reforms over the past several years. The two world organizations suggest that Latin America must seize this opportunity to design and implement better public policies to achieve their long-term objectives—economic and social development. To improve the quality of life and reduce poverty and inequality, efforts may include: creating quality jobs; consolidating fiscal systems that are solid, transparent and fair; investing in education and training; increasing the efficiency of infrastructure investment; and supporting innovation and productive development (OECD and United Nations 2012).

Taking the advantage of significant national fiscal and monetary stimuli during the financial crisis, several countries in the Latin American region are currently in an expansionary phase. The resources provided present an excellent opportunity to reform three key priority areas, education, infrastructure, and innovation, to raise future competitiveness and social inclusion (OECD and United Nations 2012). One caution is the expanding trade with China, which more than tripled during the 2000s. Although it facilitated the region's quick recovery, it also makes the region more exposed to a potential growth slowdown in China (OECD and United Nations 2012).

The next chapter will give a brief background and qualitative analysis of the 2008 global financial crisis as it relates to these six countries as a whole and individually.

Chapter 2
Impact of the 2008 Global Financial Crisis

This chapter first describes the common features of the Latin American countries reported in this booklet; next it graphically compares the GDP growth, total general government debt, unemployment rate, and consumer price inflation of the six economies during 2005–2010; and then it elaborates on the impact of the 2008 global financial crisis on each country individually.

The 2008 financial crisis, which originated from the U.S. sub-prime crisis, rapidly developed and spread into a global economic shock and economies worldwide slowed. With the U.S. and the EU dip into recession, the world economy lost two of the main drivers of international trade. As a result, in the first quarter of 2009 global nominal trade fell by 30 % on average relative to a year before (Arguello 2009). Latin America was impacted very hard in terms of loss of access to the international capital markets. Real GDP growth of the region slowed by around 8 % points, from positive growth of around 6 % in 2007 to negative GDP growth of about 2.5 % in 2009 (Porzecanski 2009). Although the Latin American countries were not immune from the strains of this financial crisis as stocks plummeted, borrowing costs rose and foreign reserves dropped (Faga 2008), the region in general weathered the crisis relatively well mainly for the following reasons.

Between 1945 and 2008, financial crises were frequent in Latin America; Argentina went through four banking crises, Brazil suffered three, and Chile, Colombia, and Mexico experienced two (Bleger 2011). The severity of the Latin American banking crises of the 1990s and 2000s led public opinion and national leadership to review existing regulations, improve banking supervision, and strengthen the local institutions in charge of these tasks. As a result, Latin America faced this global financial crisis without a single case of domestic banking crisis (Bleger 2011). In fact, this global financial crisis served as a test of the financial rules set by these six countries.

Another reason is because Eastern Europe and Asia have been the favored destinations of global foreign investment in recent years; hot money did not pour into Latin America and therefore was not suddenly withdrawn when the market panicked (Faga 2008). The region also is less economically dependent on the US, except Mexico. Latin America's exports to the U.S. have dropped from 57 % of

C. Y.-Y. Lin et al., *National Intellectual Capital and the Financial Crisis in Argentina, Brazil, Chile, Colombia, Mexico, and Venezuela*, SpringerBriefs in Economics,
DOI: 10.1007/978-1-4614-8921-4_2, © The Author(s) 2014

the region's total exports in 2000 to 40 % in 2007; yet trade with Asia increases from 4 to almost 10 % in the same periods (Faga 2008).

The 2008 global financial crisis was viewed as greater in both scope and effect for emerging economies than the East Asian financial crisis of 1997 and 1998 or the Latin American debt crisis of 2001 and 2002 (Nanto 2009). At onset all major indicators in Latin America fell sharply in the fourth quarter of 2008, including regional stock indexes fell by over half from June to October 2008. Currencies followed suit and depreciated suddenly from investor flight to the U.S. dollar reflecting a lack of confidence in local currencies. In addition, there was a reduction in workers' remittances sent from the U.S. and elsewhere, a drop in foreign tourist arrivals, and a disruption of external finance supporting foreign trade and domestic activities (Nanto 2009; Porzecanski 2009). National governments are relying on monetary, fiscal, and exchange rate policies to stimulate their economies. For this region, the IMF created a Flexible Credit Line for loans to be disbursed when the need arises rather than the traditional IMF-supported programs. Under this facility, the IMF board has approved a loan of U.S.$47 billion for Mexico and US$10.5 billion for Colombia (Nanto 2009). Among the countries adopting a fiscal stimulus, their size ranges from 2.5 % GDP in Mexico to 6.0 % in Argentina, and 8.5 % in Brazil (Nanto 2009). Direct government spending was the primary vehicle for fiscal stimulus (except Venezuela), with Brazil devoted 20 % for tax cuts and increased benefits (Nanto 2009). Apparently, the governments' stimulus policies worked and most economies in the region gradually resumed to their order, some even become stronger after the financial crisis, such as Brazil.

As of mid-2012, the sovereign debt problems continued to ail the Euro zone. In September 2011, OECD reported that major economies were tilting back into recession. The impact of the 2008 global financial crisis on each country can be easily observed from the following four graphs, namely the percentage of real GDP growth per capita, total general government debt percentage of GDP, unemployment rate of labor force, and consumer price inflation from 2005 to 2010.

Comparisons of the Six Countries

Figure 2.1 shows that all six countries had an obvious GDP growth decline in 2009, with Argentina still retaining positive growth and Mexico having the largest slide. In 2010, all but Venezuela had a clear financial recovery. Argentina and Brazil marked over 7 % rebound, yet Venezuela still had a negative growth.

In terms of the total general government debt as a percentage of the GDP, Fig. 2.2 indicates that government debt is relatively stable in these countries, with only Argentina having a sharp decrease over the 6 years. Brazil maintained a similar level, with a little increase in 2009 and then a decrease in 2010 to lower than its 2006 debt level (2005 data missing). Chile carried the lowest government debt, under 10 %; however, its debt showed a continuous increase from 2008 onward. Colombia maintained a relatively stable government debt level through

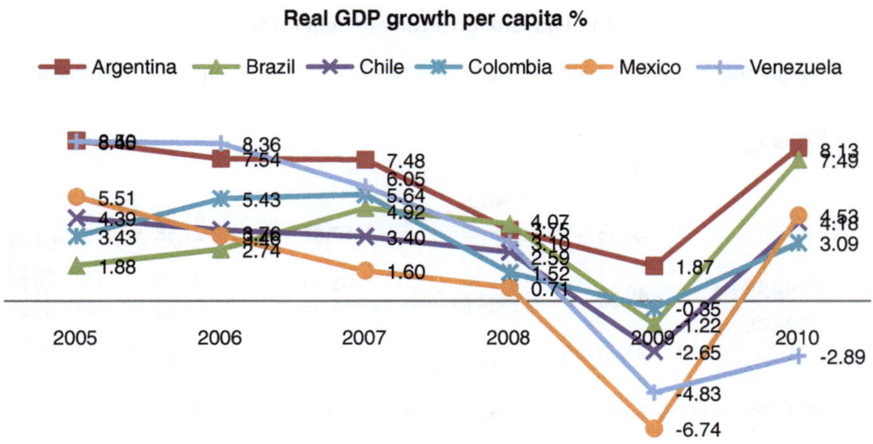

Fig. 2.1 Real GDP Growth per capita for Argentina, Brazil, Chile, Colombia, Mexico, and Venezuela from 2005 to 2010

the 6 years, with a little decrease after the financial crisis. Mexico had government debt increase in 2008 and 2009, then a slight decrease in 2010. Surprisingly, Venezuela had the largest scale government debt increase after the financial crisis in this country cluster, even after the rebound of oil price. Venezuela has the largest oil reserves in the world, with oil products accounting for about 95 % of its export earnings and contributing to around 30 % of its GDP (CIA 2012). With the oil price having doubled (from around US$40 in 2008 to around US$80 per barrel in late 2009), its government debt should be less after the financial crisis; yet Fig. 2.2 shows the contrary. However, its 24.89 % government debt of the GDP in 2010 is lower than its 2005 debt of 33.05 %.

Reinhart and Rogoff (2009) reported findings from their research on financial crises over the last 800 years that the aftermath of a financial crisis brings slow and halted growth, sustained high unemployment, and surging public debt—with the overhang of public and private debt being the most important impediment to a normal recovery from the recession.

As for the unemployment rate, Fig. 2.3 shows that all six countries had unemployment rate decreases over the 6 years, except Mexico. Comparing the last 3 years (2008, 2009, and 2010), there was a general trend of unemployment rate increase in 2009 and then a decrease in 2010, reflecting the impact of financial crisis and the region's recovery in 2010.

Figure 2.4 shows three different patterns of consumer price inflation (CPI) development for the six countries. Argentina by itself showed one pattern with a clear CPI dip in 2009. Brazil, Colombia, and Mexico had another type with relatively stable CPI over the 6 years. Chile and Venezuela shared a similar pattern, only with a wide gap between them. Their CPI gradually rose from 2005 to a peak in 2008, slid to a trough in 2009, and then rose a little bit in 2010. Although the

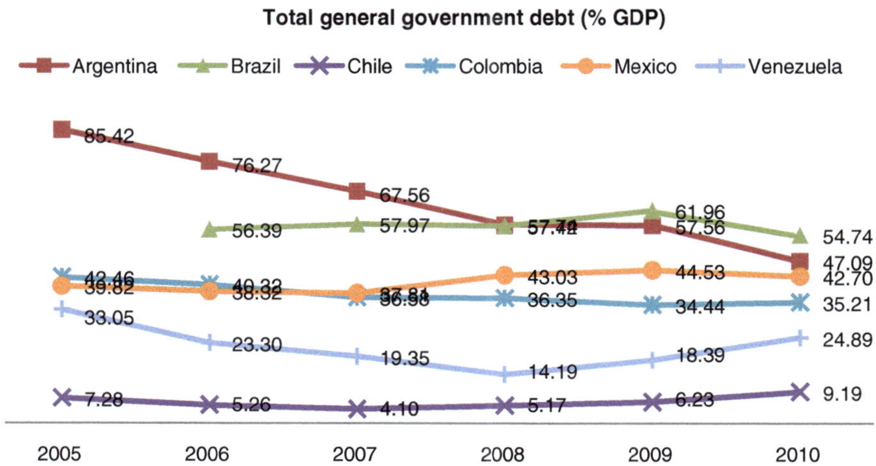

Fig. 2.2 Total General Government Debt (% of GDP) of Argentina, Brazil, Chile, Colombia, Mexico, and Venezuela from 2005 to 2010

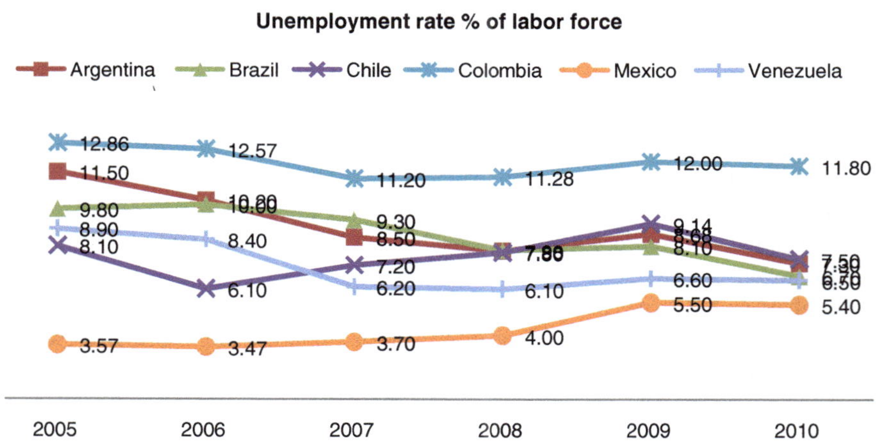

Fig. 2.3 Unemployment rate percentage of labor force in Argentina, Brazil, Chile, Colombia, Mexico, and Venezuela from 2005 to 2010

pattern is the same, the two countries had around 10–20 % points difference, with Venezuela having the highest CPI in the cluster.

In general, Figs. 2.1, 2.2, 2.3, and 2.4 for the six Latin American countries show that among the four indicators, only the real GDP growth has clear fluctuations and unemployment rate rose a little in 2009 reflecting the impact of the 2008 global financial crisis. The most unexpected findings are the exceptionally high consumer price inflation of around 30 % in more recent years in Venezuela and the low general government debt of less than 10 % in Chile.

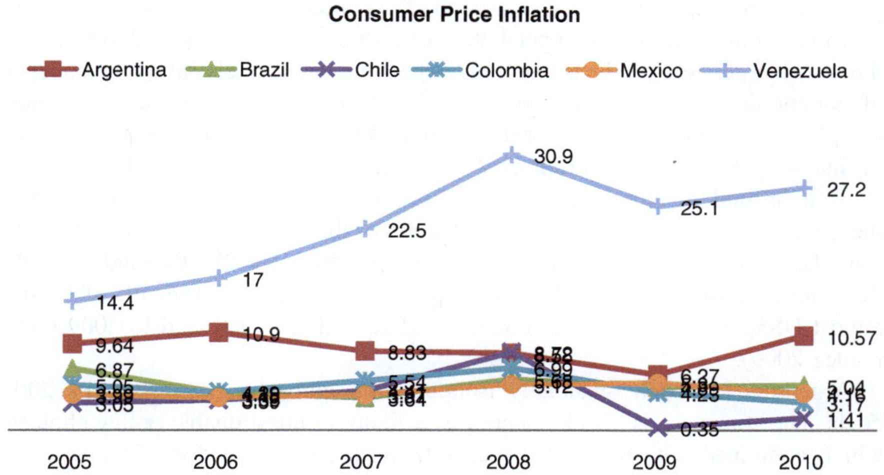

Fig. 2.4 Consumer Price Inflation of Argentina, Brazil, Chile, Colombia, Mexico, and Venezuela from 2005 to 2010

In what follows, we briefly described the impact of 2008 global financial crisis on Argentina, Brazil, Chile, Colombia, Mexico, and Venezuela in sequence. Please note that the reported amount of stimulus package was based on the exchange rate at the time of each stimulus, and thus varies. In addition, the depth of the report depends on the English literature availability for each country. Readers can refer to Appendix 1 for details on the stimulus package which each country adopted and Appendix 2 for the important meetings conducted by key global leaders during the 2008 financial crisis.

Argentina

Argentina suffered during most of the twentieth century from recurring economic crises, persistent fiscal and current account deficits, high inflation, mounting external debt, and capital flight (CIA 2012; Gutierrez 2011). A severe depression in the most serious economic, social, and political crisis in the country's turbulent history occurred in 2001 and its economy bottomed out in 2002, with real GDP 18 % smaller than in 1998 and almost 60 % of Argentines under the poverty line (Gutierrez, 2011). However, its real GDP rebounded by an average of 8.5 % annually over the subsequent 6 years with increasing inflation until the outbreak of the global financial crisis in 2008 (CIA 2012; ILO 2010a).

At first, the government and most analysts thought that Argentina would be insulated from the crisis and even benefited from it (Bermudez 2009). Then the recession hit and agricultural exports declined, followed by a severe nation-wide draught (Brown 2009). Argentina, because of its shaky economic and financial position at the outset of the crisis, was poorly positioned to deal with a protracted downturn compared to most other Latin American countries (Nanto 2009). Being the world largest soy products exporter, Argentina was severely hit by the collapse of commodity prices in late 2008 with diminished export and fiscal revenues. Coupled with the declines in investment and domestic consumer demand, sources of financing dried up, industrial activity slowed, and capital took flight.

To help fund the federal government's social security system, in October 2008, the government announced the nationalization of the private pension system, with a market value of US$25 billion or 8 % of Argentina's GDP (Bermudez 2009). This move caused a severe flight of capital in the fourth quarter of 2008 with almost US$6.65 billion left the country and such flight continued to 2009 (Bermudez 2009).

Argentina has been financially isolated from global markets since its 2001 crisis. The country was also hampered by a litany of questionable policy choices, which combined with the global recession further diminished confidence in its financial system. Although the banks remained liquid and solvent, the stock market fell at one point by 37 % and the currency has depreciated by 20 % from September 2008, in spite of exchange rate intervention (Nanto 2009). Other problems included price controls, high export taxes, and nationalization of private pension funds to bolster public finances (Nanto 2009).

To cope with the recession, Argentina conducted two bond swaps (with 15.4 % yields) for guaranteed loans that matured between 2009 and 2011 and implemented a large fiscal stimulus equal to 9 % of its GDP focused almost entirely on public works spending (Nanto 2009). Its major structural policies was the renationalization of the pension system and temporary measures aimed at providing relief to specific industries, maintaining employment, and protecting vulnerable people (ILO 2010a). Resources doubled for projects to finance housing, hospitals, roads, and sanitary systems. Other fiscal measures focused on temporarily reducing the tax and social security burden on businesses. Tax credits were offered to firms that invest in capital goods and infrastructure, with a significant part targeted at small- and medium-sized enterprises, and employers have been granted reductions in their mandatory contributions (75 % during the first year and 50 % during the second year) for new or previously undeclared employees (ILO 2010a). As of September 2009, 169,000 contributors complied and 330,547 employees had been registered under the plan (ILO 2010a).

According to International Labor Organization (ILO 2010a), Argentina's Training and Employment Insurance assisted unemployed households with education, training, workfare, and self-employment opportunities. In October 2009, the program further extended child benefits to unregistered workers earning less than the minimum wage, the unemployed, domestic workers, and self-employed workers with very low incomes. By the end of 2009, 2.7 million children and adolescents benefited, covering about 55 % of the eligible target population.

Argentina's GDP growth for 2008 was still positive at 3.8 % (ILO 2010a). Since the last quarter of 2008, reduction in consumption and export demands had a negative impact on the automotive sector, metallurgy, and textiles (CEI 2009;

Nanto 2009). In the first half of 2009, primary budget surplus was 65 % lower than in the same period in 2008, as a result of the deceleration of income expansion and of the strong increase in government expenditure, partly due to the implementation of countercyclical measures (CEI 2009). Argentina's exports declined by 21 % year-over-year in the first 6 months of 2009 (Nanto 2009). In the second quarter of 2009, GDP dropped by 0.8 % in relation to the same period in 2008 (CEI 2009). By the fourth quarter of 2009, the unemployment rate of 8.4 % was 1.1 % point above the same quarter a year earlier, mitigated by job retention measures, such as the granting of wage subsidies, shorter working hours and temporary layoffs (ILO 2010a).

In 2009, Argentina's exports to all the economic regions fell, except for those to ASEAN with an increase of 46 %. The greatest reductions were observed in sales to Brazil, the European Union and NAFTA, which, taken together, accounted for almost 60 % of its lower overall foreign sales (CEI 2009). The main origins of Argentine imports continued being Brazil, NAFTA, the European Union and China, which together represented 75 % of the total and accounted for 72 % of the import reduction. The poor external environment combined with domestic conditions resulted in a lengthy recession in Argentina, but not a major crisis (Brown 2009).

Brazil

Brazil is an upper-middle-income country which industrialized rapidly in the 1960s and 1970s under protectionist policies, yet stayed at that level in the 1980s and 1990s and remains primarily a commodity exporter (Dahlman 2009). It is the largest, most populous, and the leading economic power in South America. After record growth in 2007 and 2008, the onset of the global financial crisis hit Brazil in September 2008, as global demand for Brazil's commodity-based exports dwindled and external credit dried up (CIA 2012). However, Brazil only experienced a recession for roughly two quarters and was one of the first emerging markets to begin a recovery when improvements began emerging in the second quarter of 2009 (Mendonça 2010).

Before the crisis, Brazil had foreign reserves of US$205 billion in 2008, banks had very low foreign liabilities, only 30 % of bank assets were foreign-owned; all banks had complied with an 11 % capital requirement since 1995 (higher than the 8 % ratio usually recommended by the Basel agreements), and property loans only accounted for 2.3 % of the GDP in December 2008 (Cárdenas 2008; Mendonça 2010). These positive features indicated that the economy was protected from the credit contraction in international financial markets. However, nearly half of Brazil's exports are commodities, which are sensitive to global supply and demand. As a result between January and September of 2009, goods exports slid by 25.9 % from the previous year and exports of manufactured and semi-manufactured goods slumped by 32 and 30.8 %, respectively (ECLAC 2009). In addition, stock prices declined 20 % and spreads on Brazilian debt rose by more than 170 basis points (Cárdenas 2008). Nevertheless, Brazil also had good central bank leadership that had helped to maintain confidence in the financial system in the face of rising defaults and declining balance sheet quality (Nanto 2009).

In responding to the downturn, Brazil enacted a sizeable fiscal stimulus around 8.5 % of GDP aimed at inflation control, higher investment, a floating exchange rate, prudent management of public finances, and the fiscal measures for sustained economic growth (Mendonça 2010; Nanto 2009). Tax cuts and direct government spending were also credited with ameliorating the effects of the global downturn. Its strong institutional framework and a cautious monetary policy had curbed its inflation with a downward trend (Mendonça 2010). To boost investments, the government increased capital spending and investment in infrastructure and energy, as well as started up an extensive program of government incentives and subsidies for housing construction (Cárdenas 2008). Capital controls, temporary currency swap arrangements with the U.S. Federal Reserve, and increased U.S. dollar reserves were main measures implemented in an effort to limit the appreciation of Brazilian currency (Nanto 2009).

Three major reasons contributed to Brazil resisting the global downturn better than many other countries, according to OECD (Gurria 2009 and Nanto 2009). First, its sound policies developed over recent years and an improved balance of payments made its economy more resilient to external impact. Second, the policies centered on inflation, a floating exchange rate, prudent management of public finances, and the fiscal measures during the crisis were appropriate. Particularly, Brazil's *real* appreciated against the U.S. dollar, fully recovering the country's 2008 losses. Third, Brazilian exports began to enjoy a positive effect from the commodity price rebound and the strong recovery of the Chinese economy. In 2009, China was the largest trade partner of Brazil and was the destination for 13 % of its national exports (Mendonça 2010). Furthermore, Brazil has a large internal market and was well-positioned on the macroeconomic front, which has helped soften the effects of the global financial crisis (Nanto 2009). As a result, Brazilian government debt was upgraded from speculative to investment grade by the major ratings agencies in September 2009, lending further support for confidence in the country's financial and economic outlook (Nanto 2009).

In summary, the swift and comprehensive coping measures, including monetary and financial policy, exchange-rate and foreign-trade policy, sectoral policies, labor and social policies, and fiscal policy (Valadao and Porto 2009) of the Brazilian government helped minimize the negative influence of the 2008 global financial crisis.

Chile

Chile has a market-oriented economy characterized by a high level of foreign trade, a reputation for strong financial institutions, and sound policy that have won it the strongest sovereign bond rating in South America. Exports account for more than one-fourth of its GDP, with commodities making up about three-quarters of total exports. Copper alone provides one-third of government revenue (CIA 2012). During the early 1990s, the democratic government deepened the economic reform and Chile became known as a role model for economic reform. Chile experienced 12 magnificent years from 1986 until 1997, when GDP grew more than 7 % per year, opening up the country to the rest of the world, creating jobs, and strengthening macroeconomic balances (Barton and Krell 2011). However, impacted by the Asian financial crisis of 1998, Chile lived through 12 lean years afterwards. The rate of growth and employment both went down by half; growth has averaged 4 % per year since 1999 (Barton and Krell 2011).

Chile enhanced its longstanding commitment to trade liberalization with the signing of 57 free trade agreements including the U.S., the European Union, the Common Market of the South America, China, India, South Korea, and Mexico (CIA 2012). Exports accounted for 44 % of its GDP in 2008. Because of its high trade and capital market integration, the economy was severely affected by the financial crisis. Export volume dropped by nearly 20 % and industrial production fell by 9.3 % during the first half of 2009 (Briones 2010). In the Latin American region, Chile was the most affected country by the 2008 global financial crisis (Briones 2010). As a result, its unemployment rate grew from 7.5 % in 2008 to 10.8 % during the second quarter of 2009 (Briones 2010). Inflation rose from an average of 2.6 % in 2006 to 7.8 % in 2008, with a peak of 9.9 % in October 2008 (Briones 2010).

Chilean stimulus was planned according to the four pillars of incentives, namely government spending and investment, expanding credit access for companies, support to largely low-income people, and employment protection and incentives for worker training (Briones 2010). In January 2009, the Chilean central bank began an aggressive expansionary monetary policy and committed itself to provide liquidity to the market. On January 5th, 2009, the government launched its major fiscal stimulus package of US$4 billion (2.8 % of its GDP and 14 % of planned current fiscal expenditures), based on a mixture of fiscal spending and temporary tax reductions (Briones 2010). The plan was then complemented by a national agreement on labor market assistance, job protection, and job-training stimulus. Fiscal policy was at the core of the Chilean government response to the crisis, which had a mixture of new fiscal spending, mainly targeted at low-income households (US$1.1 billion), investment (US$1.7 billion), and tax cuts, including specific tax cuts in the credit market, the advancement of planned tax credits, and a temporary reduction in provisional monthly tax prepayments for companies (US$1.1 billion) (Briones 2010).

Later in May 2009, the government launched supplementary fiscal policies including cash stipends of about $70 (Chilean Peso 40,000) for 1.7 million poor families that benefited more than 4 million people (Briones 2010). In addition, the government introduced insurance mechanisms for higher education financing and mortgage dividends and injected US$500 million in fresh capital into the state bank Banco Estado to provide credit to small and medium-sized companies. As a result, more than 100,000 jobs were created by such investment plan (Briones 2010).

Furthermore, the government implemented subventions for low-income young unskilled workers, a group in which the unemployment rate is three times higher than the national average. An extension of unemployment insurance for workers with temporary work contracts was launched. A law was also enacted on May 28th, 2009 that provided tax reductions to companies retaining workers (Briones 2010), with the tripartite agreement between government, workers' unions, and companies. It also offered incentives for worker training, by granting workers a special authorization to undertake training outside their own firms.

In addition, the government advanced to 2009 a pension reform originally announced for 2010, which benefited 950,000 retired people by increasing the amount of their basic retirement pensions (Briones 2010). By June 2009, 51.6 % of the fiscal budget and 58.4 % of the stimulus plan had already been implemented and the estimated cost of the tax elimination for 2009 (in terms of lost fiscal revenues) was $628 million (0.4 % of GDP) (Briones 2010).

In the past, the Chilean government conducted a rule-based countercyclical fiscal policy, accumulating surpluses in sovereign wealth funds during periods of high copper prices and economic growth, and allowing deficit spending only during periods of low copper prices and growth. As of September 2008, those sovereign wealth funds—kept mostly outside the country and separate from Central Bank reserves—amounted to more than US$20 billion (CIA 2012). Chile used US$4 billion from this fund to finance a fiscal stimulus package to fend off the 2008 recession with great speed and efficiency (Hutchinson 2009).

Colombia

Colombia is the third largest exporter of oil to the U.S. (CIA 2012). Therefore, it was extremely vulnerable to the financial crisis that originated in the U.S. Before the crisis, Colombia was already growing at slower rates. In 2008, it was only 2.5 % with a negative growth (−0.7 %) in the last quarter of that year. Growth in every sector decreased over the same period of 2007, except for mining (Reinoso 2010). Its weakening export performance started in late 2008 as a result of the decreased demand from its four major trade partners: The U.S., the European Union, Ecuador, and Venezuela. These four countries accounted for 70 % of its exports, more than half (37 %) of which went to the U.S. (Reinoso 2010). In addition, Colombia had been affected by Venezuela's trade embargo since mid-2009, caused by a diplomatic dispute over the U.S. military presence in Colombia. Venezuela's share in exports fell from 18 to 4 %. Colombia reported a loss of 170,000 jobs due to the trade embargo (Reinoso 2010).

The financial crisis led Colombia into a recession. Industrial production in April 2009 decreased 14.5 %, hitting a record low over 10 years (Xinhua 2009). Exports fell 12.7 % on average and FDI decreased by 18.6 %, while lending rates soared (Reinoso 2010). The appreciation of the Colombian peso against the U.S. dollar also affected its exports. The Colombian central bank cut the basic interest rate seven times between December 2008 and July 2009 to prevent the crisis from further deepening and to boost economic growth (Xinhua 2009). In March 2009, a system of soft loans up to US$260 million for companies affected by falling external demand and the exchange rate appreciation was implemented, in particular for automotive and household appliances (Reinoso 2010). The IMF also decided to provide a loan of US$10.5 billion to help Colombia weather the crisis (Xinhua 2009).

In coping with the economic downturn, the Colombian government implemented four strategies, including taking a countercyclical fiscal stance, especially prioritizing public expenditure to infrastructure programs; guaranteeing access to external financing; ensuring domestic financing of productive activity; and protecting jobs and promoting competitiveness (Reinoso 2010). Other measures covered food subsidies and the strengthening of credit programs for rural producers (Reinoso 2010). Through the Fund for Financing the Agricultural Sector, the government provided producers in crisis with credit lines for approximately US$1.7 million dollars. Another Rural Capitalization Incentive (RCI) program is used to promote modernization and provide support to exports, for example improving product traceability (Reinoso 2010).

With fiscal structure deteriorated in the mid 1990s, Colombia was limited in using the fiscal policy as a tool for short-term economic stabilization in the downturn of 2008 and 2009 (Economy Watch 2010). However, the government still carried out a reasonable countercyclical fiscal policy, in addition to maintain the conditions for debt sustainability, and giving priority to infrastructure expenses and to social and productive support programs. It assured external financing for 2009 by allocating US$2,400 million from multilateral banks and US$1,000 million from the issuance of a global bond in the international capital markets. The authorities also facilitated financing the production activity of small companies by US$650 million from development bank, US$300 million from CAF-Bancoldex, and US$31 million from National Guarantee Fund for capitalization.

During the financial crisis, trade protection was increased in agriculture. For industry, government effort was placed on promoting competitiveness such as offsetting the appreciation of the Colombian peso and the credit squeeze (Reinoso 2010). Thus, policies were aimed at credit easing through development banks and lowering taxes in order to reduce costs. To promote competitiveness, tariffs were also eliminated on a temporary basis on a large number of imports and capital goods not produced at home. In the case of final goods, quotas were imposed to protect textiles and footwear from Chinese imports (Reinoso 2010).

Colombian unemployment rose to 12.1 % in April 2009 and as many as 2.54 million Colombians were out of work—211,000 more than a year previous (Xinhua 2009). Throughout 2009, the economy remained in recession and was kept afloat by government spending with the growth of about 0.5 % (Alsema 2009; Reinoso 2010). In general, the IMF executive directors praised the Colombian economic authorities for using adequate macroeconomic policies and for the wide range of structural reforms, which contributed to accelerate its growth and decreased its vulnerability (Ministry of Finance and Public Credit, 2009).

Mexico

The Mexican economy experienced moderately strong growth during the pre-crisis period of 2004–2007, as real GDP expanded by about 4 % a year (ILO 2010c). However, almost 80 % of Mexico's total exports were destined for the U.S., of which a considerable proportion was durable goods, making the country susceptible to the U.S. economic downturn (Sidaoui, Ramos-Francia and Cuadra 2010; Villarreal 2010). Up until mid-September 2008, the financial conditions and economic activity in Mexico had not been severely affected by the late 2007 financial stress and economic slowdown (CIA 2012; Sidaoui, Ramos-Francia and Cuadra 2010), then the financial crisis deepened and hit Mexico hard and fast (Nanto 2009).

Mexico faced two adverse shocks of considerable magnitude: A collapse in export demand and substantial constraints in accessing international financial markets (Sanchez 2010; Sidaoui, Ramos-Francia and Cuadra 2010). In addition, there was high corporate exposure to foreign currency through complex derivatives instruments. At the outset, Mexico experienced a run on the peso, which caused its value to fall at one point by 40 % from its August 2008 high (Nanto 2009). To cope with the crisis, the Mexican government adopted supportive monetary and fiscal policies. The central government has increased liquidity in the banking system, including multiple cuts in the prime policy lending rate and increased its credit lines with the World Bank, International Monetary Fund, and Inter-American Development Bank (Nanto 2009). In addition, a foreign currency swap line with the U.S. Federal Reserve for up to US$30 billion was agreed on October 29, 2008 (Nanto 2009; Sidaoui, Ramos-Francia and Cuadra 2010).

Amid national and international economic uncertainty, the Mexican GDP began to contract in the second and third quarters of 2008 with a growth of about 1.5 % in 2008 (ILO 2010c). By mid-2009, the economic recession had turned out to be deeper and oil prices were lower than anticipated, resulting in a substantial decline in public sector revenues (Sidaoui, Ramos-Francia and Cuadra 2010). In the first quarter of 2009, output was down by 6.9 % compared with the previous quarter (ILO 2010c), in the second quarter the total export of goods and services was 24 % lower than their peak level six quarters earlier (Sanchez 2010); Mexico's GDP contracted by 6.6 % in 2009, the sharpest decline of any Latin American economy

(CIA 2012; Nanto 2009; Villarreal 2010). Its decline in GDP reflects a number of factors, including lower oil prices, reduced exports, the outbreak of H1N1 influenza, declining tourism, and lower remittances from workers abroad (Heritage 2012c; ILO 2010c). The Mexican government depends heavily on oil revenues, which provide 30 to 40 % of the government's fiscal revenues and remittance inflows (largely from the U.S.) are Mexico's second-highest source of foreign currency after oil (Villarreal 2010). Mexico's Central Bank reported that remittance inflows fell 16.0 % in 2009 to US$21.1 billion, which had mostly affected the poor (Villarreal 2010).

The Mexican economy contracted for four consecutive quarters beginning in the fourth quarter of 2008, the worst recession in 6 decades (Nanto 2009). The country's fiscal position weakened because oil revenues fell, partly due to the drop in international energy prices and the decline in domestic oil production (Sidaoui, Ramos-Francia and Cuadra 2010). It also experienced liquidity problems and a loss in investor confidence as a result of large losses on corporate foreign exchange positions in 2008 and the uncertainty over the outbreak of the H1N1 virus in mid-2009 (Villarreal 2010). Total FDI flows to Mexico decreased by 42.5 %, from $24.3 billion in 2008 to $12.2 billion in 2009 (Villarreal 2010). However, the Mexican economy was most deeply disturbed through the real sector, especially the contraction of goods and services to and from the U.S. (Sanchez 2010).

The recession led to a loss of formal employment and by June 2009 the number of formal full-time and temporary workers registered had declined by 596,200 compared with a year earlier, of which 94.4 % were full-time workers (ILO 2010c). The downturn pushed up unemployment to a historic high of 6.3 % in August 2009, or nearly 3 million people (ILO 2010c). Increasing unemployment throughout the country led to a growing trend toward informality and self-employment, which resulted in increased poverty levels, diminished productivity, and lower prospects for sustained economic growth (Villarreal 2010).

Mexico's fiscal stimulus amounted to 2.5 % of its GDP and was targeted on infrastructure spending and subsidies for key goods of household budgets (Nanto 2009). Government programs to support small and medium-sized businesses, worker training, employment generation, and social safety nets have been expanded (Nanto 2009). In early 2008, the Mexican government created the National Infrastructure Fund and the Program of Support to the Economy, Investment and Employment to form Mexico's countercyclical policy strategy together with an increased Federal Budget (ILO 2010c). Approximately US$80 billion was allocated by various organizations for infrastructure, employment, households, and small and medium-sized enterprises (SMEs). Readers can refer to Appendix 1 for stimulus package details. The National Program of Infrastructure provided about half of the stimulus to foster public and private investment of US$40.4 billion (570 billion pesos) in 2009 (ILO 2010c). Faced with a significant deterioration of global growth, especially in the U.S., an additional Program to Boost Growth and Employment provided a fiscal stimulus to the economy of US$6.39 billion (90.3 billion Mexican pesos) in October 2008, equivalent to 0.7 % of its GDP (ILO 2010c). Mexico's development banks also contributed an additional amount of up to US$2.48 billion (35 billion pesos) to boost SME development (ILO 2010c).

In early January 2009, the National Agreement for Family Economy and Employment (ANEFE) put into effect 25 measures to protect Mexican employment and the economy. These were grouped into five areas: Support for employment and workers; support to families and households; support for competitiveness and SMEs; investment in infrastructure for competitiveness and employment; and promotion of a transparent and efficient public spending (ILO 2010c). Growth in GDP returned in the second quarter of 2009 and picked up later that year (ILO 2010c).

Venezuela

Venezuela remains highly dependent on oil revenues, which account for roughly 95 % of its export earnings, about 55 % of the federal budget revenues, and around 30 % of its GDP (CIA 2012). In 2007, Venezuela topped most nations in the world and the entire American Hemisphere (including the U.S. and Canada) with the biggest international reserves per capita—a total US$34 billion reserves and US$1,300 per capita (Saatdjian 2008). Fueled by high oil prices, record government spending helped boost the GDP by about 10 % in 2006, 8 % in 2007, and nearly 5 % in 2008, before a sharp drop in oil prices in 2009 and 2010 (CIA 2012; Weisbrot 2010a). However, the country's high level of inflation, averaging 30 % in 2008, 27 % in 2009, and 28 % in 2010, had also eroded purchasing power (Sullivan 2011). In the fourth quarter of 2008, world oil prices suddenly collapsed, falling in 6 months from a peak of US$137 to just US$41. This undermined governmental capacity to continue its spending spree in the social sector (Anees 2010; Weisbrot 2010b).

Venezuela was one of the Latin American countries that experienced acute economic hardships during the global financial crisis (Rodriguez 2011). Earnings from oil production dropped by 51.9 % from US$28.597 million in the second quarter of 2008 to only US$13.576 million in the same period of 2009 (Larsen 2009). Its 2008 FDI fell by 18 % compared a year earlier (Larsen 2009). General Motors, which supplies Venezuela with 40 % of all its vehicles, closed all its production plants for 3 months with the effect that thousands of workers were temporarily laid off (Larsen 2009). The economy shrank by 3.3 % in 2009, worse than the record for the total of Latin American countries of 2.4 % (Vera Azaf 2010; Weisbrot 2010a). The slowdown was probably due to government efforts to slow inflation in 2007 (Weisbrot, Ray and Sandoval 2009). However, in terms of lost jobs, Venezuela showed only a moderate increase of around 0.5 % in the rate of unemployment in 2009 (Vera Azaf 2010). Firms in the agribusiness, banking, tourism, oil, cement, steel sectors, petroleum, communications, and electricity sectors were nationalized by Chavez regime in 2008 and 2009 (Anees 2010). Despite the country's sizeable surplus, it still faced significant economic challenges, some of which had been worsened by mistaken macroeconomic policy choices; therefore, the country was said not facing a crisis, but rather a policy choice (Vera Azaf 2010; Weisbrot 2010a).

When oil prices collapsed in the last quarter of 2008, the government did not expand public spending to provide a strong fiscal stimulus. Instead, public sector growth fell off sharply, increasing by only 0.9 % in 2009, compared to 16.3 % in 2008 (Weisbrot 2010b). During the 2008 global financial crisis, the problem Venezuela encountered was different from that of other countries. The most important, and practically the only, direct impact of these external events on Venezuela was through oil prices. In 2009, its current account deficit of 2 and 3 % of the GDP and low foreign public debt at about 9.8 % of the GDP were not significant in the face of its large reserves (Weisbrot, Ray and Sandoval 2009). Venezuela ran a current account surplus estimated at 13.9 % of its GDP for 2008 and had approximately US$82 billion, or 25 % of its GDP—more than twice what the country needs (Weisbrot, Ray and Sandoval 2009).

In 2009, the Venezuelan government announced a major public spending program of about US$12 billion, or 3.6 % of the GDP (Weisbrot, Ray and Sandoval 2009). According to its Finance Minister, manufacturing, commerce and transport had been identified as areas of the economy facing difficulties and would be the targets of measures aimed at achieving "positive growth" amid the global slowdown (Morgan, n.d.)

Chapter 3
National Intellectual Capital Development of the Six Latin American Countries

In this chapter, we first present the development of national intellectual capital in the six Latin American countries over the 6 years, then graphically display the relationship between each individual capital with GDP per capita (ppp), afterward we describe the relative position of the long-term and short-term intellectual capital in these six economies and explain the dynamics of national intellectual capital for three time periods (2005–2006, 2007–2008, and 2009–2010). Finally, we illustrate the NIC trajectory of these six countries on three-dimensional (3D) landscapes showing all 48 countries.

National Intellectual Capital Development

The national intellectual capital measurement model in this study is based on the indicators described in Appendix 3, containing human capital, market capital, process capital, renewal capital, and financial capital. This model has been statistically validated for its validity and reliability; the definitions of the indicators are listed in Appendix 4. This booklet series covers a total of 48 countries in 11 country clusters (see Appendix 5 for details).

For a full picture of all the 48 countries being studied, Appendix 6 exhibits the scores and rankings of human capital, market capital, process capital, renewal capital, financial capital, and overall intellectual capital (hereafter termed NIC) covered in this booklet series. Table 3.1 summarizes the status of the six Latin American countries compared with the 48 countries reported in Appendix 6. In terms of NIC ranking, Chile ranks 30, followed by Colombia at 41, Brazil at 42, Mexico at 43, Argentina at 45, and Venezuela at 48.

Among the five types of capital, Chile is especially advanced in market capital, ranked 5 among 48 countries. Venezuela ranked last at 48 for its market capital, process capital, and NIC.

The following six figures compare human capital, market capital, process capital, renewal capital, financial capital, and NIC of the six countries. All individual capital scores are based on a 1–10 scale with the NIC score being the sum of the five capital scores.

C. Y.-Y. Lin et al., *National Intellectual Capital and the Financial Crisis in Argentina, Brazil, Chile, Colombia, Mexico, and Venezuela*, SpringerBriefs in Economics,
DOI: 10.1007/978-1-4614-8921-4_3,

Table 3.1 National intellectual capital scores and ranking of Argentina, Brazil, Chile, Colombia, Mexico, and Venezuela (2005–2010)

	Human capital		Market capital		Process capital		Renewal capital		Financial capital		NIC	
Country	Score	Ranking	Score	Ranking	Score	Ranking	Score	Ranking	Score	Ranking	Score	Ranking
Argentina	5.370	36	3.340	47	3.038	47	1.413	45	8.755	34	21.916	45
Brazil	4.757	44	4.589	38	3.076	46	1.753	36	8.481	40	22.656	42
Chile	5.414	35	6.663	5	5.163	28	1.710	37	8.784	32	27.734	30
Colombia	4.941	40	4.677	36	3.951	37	1.435	44	8.348	42	23.352	41
Mexico	4.871	42	4.491	39	3.226	45	1.237	48	8.781	33	22.606	43
Venezuela	4.884	41	2.761	48	2.545	48	1.277	46	8.625	38	20.092	48

Human Capital

National human capital mainly represents a nation's investment in nurturing qualified human resources, such as higher education enrollment, skilled labor, and public expenditure on education. It is a long-term oriented NIC (Lin and Edvinsson 2011, p 323), taking time to develop yet not susceptible to external impact. Figure 3.1 shows that human capital of these six countries is relatively stable over the studied 6 years, with Argentina and Chile having gradual progress from 2008. From 2009, human capital of these six countries formed two clusters, the high cluster contains Argentina and Chile and the low cluster the other four countries.

Market Capital

National market capital mainly represents international trade and relationships, such as cross-border ventures, globalization, and exports of goods. Figure 3.2 shows a relatively stable market capital development in each individual country. However, there is larger score variation between countries compared to human

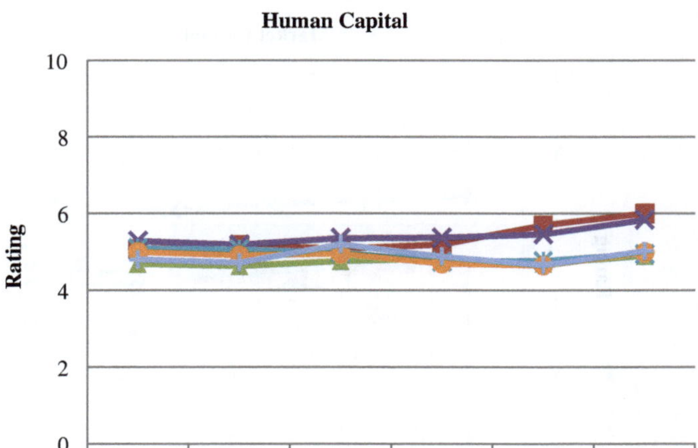

	2005	2006	2007	2008	2009	2010
Argentina	5.08	5.18	5.08	5.19	5.69	6.00
Brazil	4.69	4.64	4.76	4.84	4.71	4.91
Chile	5.29	5.18	5.36	5.37	5.46	5.83
Colombia	5.10	5.06	4.99	4.75	4.78	4.96
Mexico	5.00	4.92	4.95	4.70	4.66	4.99
Venezuela	4.82	4.73	5.19	4.88	4.66	5.02

Fig. 3.1 Human capital of the six Latin American countries

capital scores in Fig. 3.1. Chile consistently had much higher market capital than the other five countries, with a large increase in 2010. Market capital of Brazil, Colombia, and Mexico was in the middle; and that of Argentina and Venezuela in the lower level. Brazil had continuous market capital increase from 2006 onwards, irrespective to the global financial crisis. The two oil dependent countries, Mexico and Venezuela, had an obvious market capital drop in 2009, and rebounded in 2010 with the global oil price increase.

Process Capital

National process capital represents the infrastructure required for building a prosperous society, such as capital availability, mobile phone subscribers, and government efficiency. Figure 3.3 shows that consistently Chile had the highest and Colombia the second highest process capital in this country cluster. Argentina and Colombia had a similar development pattern where process capital started to decline from 2006 to 2008, and then rebounded after the financial crisis in 2009 and 2010. Brazil was relatively stable over the years, with a slight increase after the financial crisis. As in Fig. 3.2, the two oil dependent countries experienced

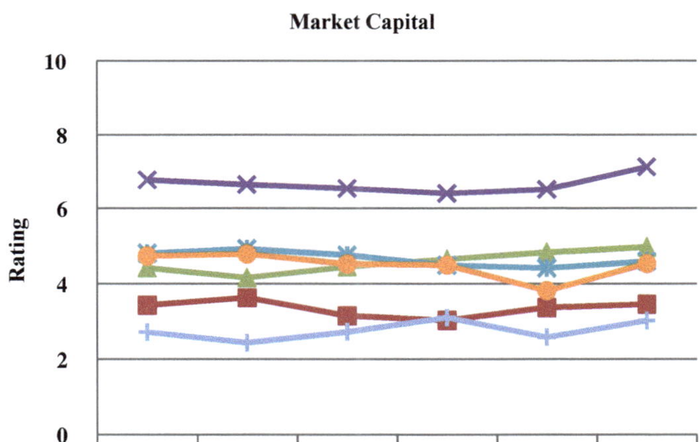

	2005	2006	2007	2008	2009	2010
Argentina	3.43	3.62	3.14	3.03	3.37	3.45
Brazil	4.43	4.17	4.46	4.66	4.84	4.98
Chile	6.77	6.64	6.53	6.40	6.51	7.13
Colombia	4.82	4.93	4.77	4.50	4.43	4.61
Mexico	4.75	4.80	4.54	4.51	3.82	4.55
Venezuela	2.72	2.43	2.72	3.10	2.58	3.02

Fig. 3.2 Market capital of the six Latin American countries

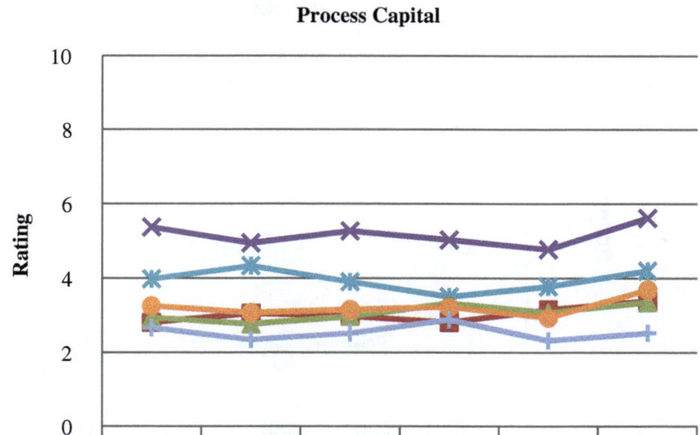

	2005	2006	2007	2008	2009	2010
Argentina	2.81	3.06	2.98	2.82	3.16	3.40
Brazil	2.94	2.77	2.98	3.32	3.09	3.36
Chile	5.37	4.94	5.26	5.03	4.77	5.62
Colombia	3.98	4.33	3.91	3.51	3.78	4.20
Mexico	3.26	3.08	3.16	3.23	2.94	3.69
Venezuela	2.67	2.34	2.52	2.89	2.32	2.53

Fig. 3.3 Process capital of the six Latin American countries

process capital declines in 2009 then rebounded in 2010, with Mexico having a more obvious recovery.

Renewal Capital

National renewal capital represents the capability of R&D and innovation, such as R&D spending, scientific articles, and patents. Figure 3.4 shows an overlapping development at the bottom 20 percentile of the graph, indicating very low renewal capital in this country cluster over the 6 years.

Financial Capital

National financial capital is the GDP per capita (ppp) in US dollars converted into a score from 1 to 10. The score conversion process is explained in Appendix 3. Figure 3.5 also shows an overlapping development, indicating the financial capital

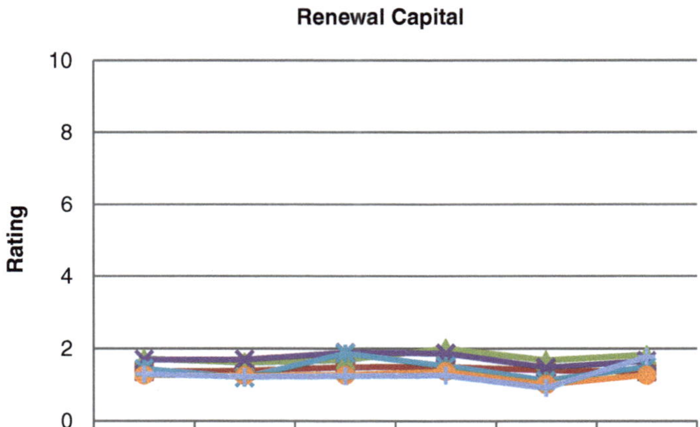

	2005	2006	2007	2008	2009	2010
Argentina	1.36	1.38	1.48	1.50	1.39	1.36
Brazil	1.72	1.61	1.68	2.01	1.67	1.83
Chile	1.69	1.69	1.88	1.87	1.48	1.65
Colombia	1.43	1.19	1.86	1.52	1.11	1.50
Mexico	1.26	1.26	1.26	1.37	1.01	1.26
Venezuela	1.29	1.22	1.23	1.25	0.91	1.77

Fig. 3.4 Renewal capital of the six Latin American countries

of the six countries does not depart too much from each other. In 2005, Mexico had the highest financial capital score; however, in 2010 Mexico became the third highest, surpassed by Argentina and Chile. In real dollars, the average GDP per capita (ppp) of 2005–2010 was US$13,506 for Argentina, US$9,982 for Brazil, US$13,853 for Chile, US$8,643 for Colombia, US$13,790 for Mexico, and US$11,663 for Venezuela.

The above analyses reveal that although Colombia ranked the second highest (next to Chile) in NIC in this country cluster, its financial capital was the lowest in terms of both the 1–10 score and the six-years average of GDP per capita (ppp) in US dollars. Such information indicates that Colombia did not capitalize on its relatively better intangible assets to generate more tangible values. In other words, the financial management of Colombia has much room for improvement.

NIC

NIC is the overall national intellectual capital containing the five types of capital discussed above. Figure 3.6 presents NIC trends with three clusters. Chile consistently is at the top; Argentina, Brazil, Colombia, and Mexico in the middle; and Venezuela at the bottom.

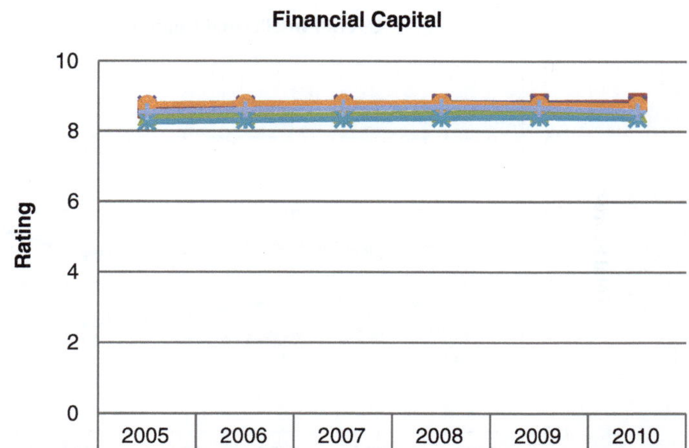

	2005	2006	2007	2008	2009	2010
Argentina	8.63	8.69	8.75	8.80	8.83	8.84
Brazil	8.41	8.44	8.47	8.52	8.52	8.52
Chile	8.74	8.76	8.79	8.82	8.81	8.79
Colombia	8.27	8.31	8.35	8.38	8.40	8.38
Mexico	8.76	8.79	8.80	8.81	8.77	8.75
Venezuela	8.55	8.61	8.66	8.69	8.66	8.57

Fig. 3.5 Financial capital of the six Latin American countries

The Relationship Between Each Individual Capital and GDP Per Capita (ppp)

We investigate the relationship between each individual capital and economic growth by using the following six figures (Figs. 3.7, 3.8, 3.9, 3.10, 3.11, and 3.12). The graphs have four dimensions: the *X* axis changes from graph to graph (NIC, human capital, market capital, process capital, and renewal capital), the *Y* axis is a fixed dimension of GDP per capita (ppp) in US dollars (hereafter termed GDP), the color shade represents renewal capital with red denoting higher levels of renewal capital, and the bubble size denoting the population of a nation. Figure 3.7 is the relationship between NIC and GDP for all 48 countries. Figures 3.8, 3.9, 3.10, 3.11,and 3.12 display the codevelopment of the intellectual capital–GDP relationship over the 6-year timeframe for the six countries. Since financial capital is a converted score from the GDP, there is no need to plot its relationship with GDP in US dollars. In the figures, 2005 is the starting point tagged with the name of the countries, and the ending point is 2010.

Figure 3.7 is particularly plotted to clearly show a full picture of the relationship between NIC and GDP for 48 countries in 2010. The strong positive correlation indicates that the higher the NIC the higher the GDP, and vice versa.

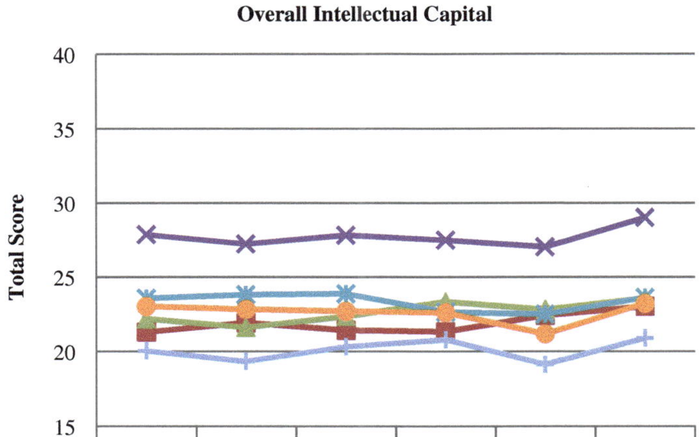

	2005	2006	2007	2008	2009	2010
Argentina	21.31	21.93	21.43	21.34	22.44	23.04
Brazil	22.19	21.62	22.35	23.34	22.82	23.60
Chile	27.85	27.21	27.82	27.48	27.02	29.02
Colombia	23.59	23.83	23.88	22.67	22.50	23.64
Mexico	23.03	22.84	22.71	22.62	21.19	23.24
Venezuela	20.04	19.34	20.32	20.81	19.14	20.91

Fig. 3.6 NIC of the six Latin American countries

Consequently, enhancing NIC is definitely a strategic issue that deserves the attention of national policy makers.

With the status of all 48 countries as the background, Fig. 3.8 indicates that NIC and GDP codevelopment of the six countries falls at the bottom left corner of the belt-shaped bubble continuum. Horizontal progress denotes NIC development, whereas vertical progress represents GDP per capita (ppp) growth. Viewing Fig. 3.8 together with Fig. 3.6 reveals that generally NIC declined during the financial crisis then rebounded after the crisis in 2010. The relatively small vertical progress as a whole indicates that the economic growth in terms of US dollars in this country cluster is small. Except Chile and Venezuela, the codevelopment paths of the other four countries fall within the continuum and overlapping with each other. The path of Chile locates at the right-hand side of the continuum, whereas that of Venezuela is at the left-hand side; which means Chile has better NIC development over its GDP per capita (ppp) growth during the 6 years and Venezuela is on the other way around.

Figure 3.9 shows that the codevelopment of human capital and GDP of the six countries is intertwined with each other and locates at the bottom level among the 48 countries. Figure 3.9 together with Fig. 3.1 shows that human capital of Argentina and Chile had relatively large-scale advancement after the financial crisis. The codevelopment path of all countries fall within the continuum indicates

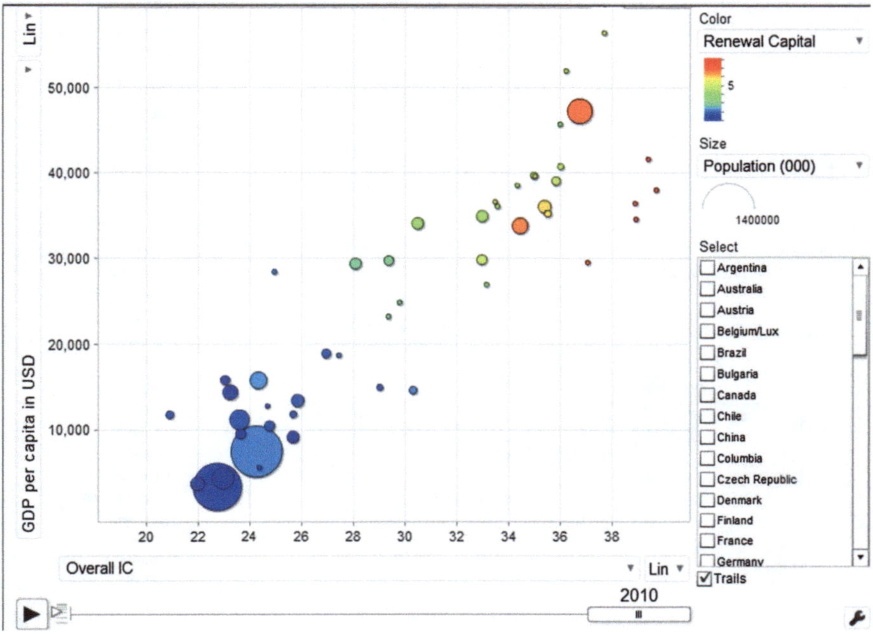

Fig. 3.7 NIC versus GDP per capita (ppp) for 48 countries in 2010

a similar pace of human capital development and GDP per capita (ppp) growth in this country cluster.

In general, the bubble formation of Fig. 3.10 is very different from that of other figures in this section, without a clear belt-shaped continuum from the bottom left to the upper right. This means that market capital is not as highly related with GDP per capita (ppp) as the other capitals are in this set of data. A further explanation is that market capital of advanced countries (generally positioned at the upper right) is not necessarily better than that of emerging countries (the two big bubbles at the bottom center are China and India).

Figure 3.10 together with Fig. 3.2 shows that market capital (*X* axis) development of the six Latin American countries is spreading across low level (Argentina and Venezuela), middle level (Brazil, Colombia, and Mexico), and high level (Chile) on the graph. However, their GDP per capita (ppp) growth (*Y* axis) is within a relatively small range. Colombia and Mexico are the two countries that had lower market capital in 2010 than in 2005. Chile has much better market capital than the other countries, however its GDP per capita (ppp) did not have much difference from that of others, indicating the adding value of its market capital needs to be improved.

In Fig. 3.11, the belt-shaped continuum appears again, indicating that process capital is highly related with GDP. The process capital and GDP per capita (ppp) codevelopment of the six countries is again at the bottom left corner of the bubble

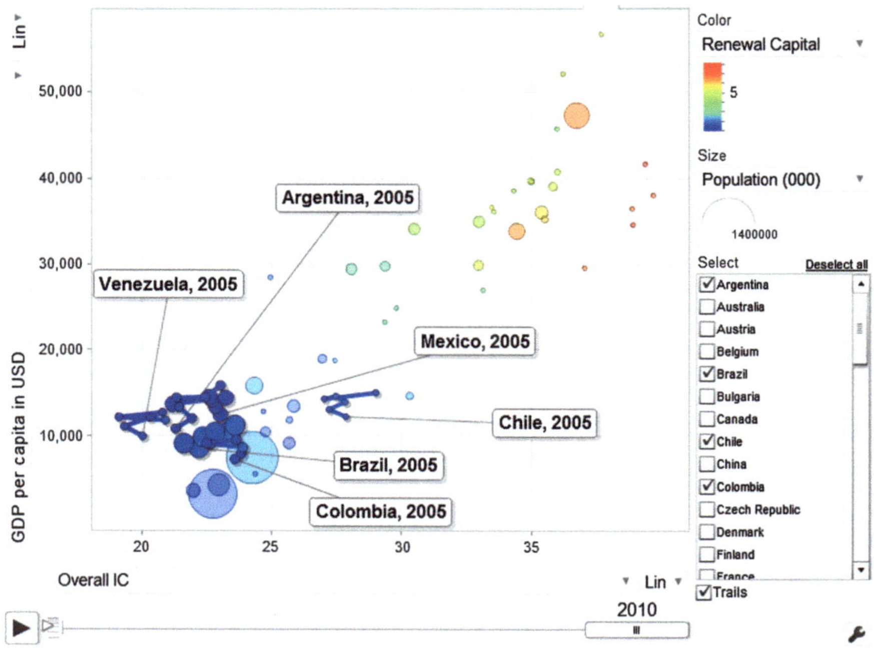

Fig. 3.8 The development of NIC and GDP per capita (ppp) for the six Latin American countries from 2005 to 2010

continuum, except Chile locates at the lower middle part. The figure also indicates that process capital of this country cluster (except Chile and Colombia) is at the very bottom of the scale, even lower than that of China and India (the two big bubbles). Figure 3.11 together with Fig. 3.3 shows that Venezuela is the only country that had process capital regress after the financial crisis.

Figure 3.12 indicates that renewal capital and GDP per capita (ppp) codevelopment of the 48 countries had two formations. The spreading formation for the advanced countries at the upper right, and the belt-shaped continuum for the less developed countries at the bottom left. That means, for advanced countries, higher renewal capital does not necessarily relate with a higher GDP per capita (ppp) and vice versa. Yet, for less developed countries, increases in renewal capital do related with a higher GDP per capita (ppp). From the formation of the bottom left continuum, it is clear that small increases in renewal capital were accompanied with relatively high GDP per capita (ppp) growth. This finding reveals a strong message that investing in renewal capital development may facilitate GDP per capita (ppp) growth for less developed countries.

The renewal capital and GDP per capita (ppp) codevelopment of the six countries is at the very bottom left corner of the graph within a very small range. Figure 3.12 together with Fig. 3.4 shows a very stable renewal capital development over the 6 years, except Brazil and Venezuela had slight progress.

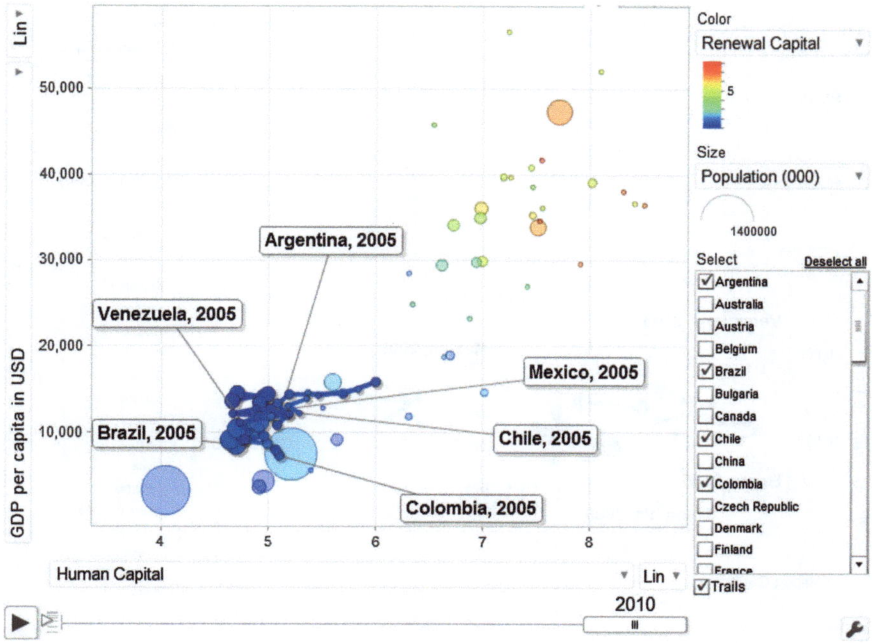

Fig. 3.9 The development of human capital and GDP per capita (ppp) for the six Latin American countries from 2005 to 2010

Long-Term and Short-Term National Intellectual Capital

In addition to the above six figures that show the relationship of each individual capital with GDP, the following four figures further plot the relationships between human capital and renewal capital, as well as between market capital and process capital. In our first study (Lin and Edvinsson 2011, p 324), we found that the combined increase in human capital and renewal capital would lead to a nation's long-term development; whereas the combined increase in market capital and process capital might result in more immediate development. To present their relationships, Figs. 3.13, 3.14, 3.15, and 3.16 map the four capitals on a coordinate with two types of presentation. Based on the same data, Figs. 3.13 and 3.15 exhibit the scatter plot for the six countries only, whereas Figs. 3.14 and 3.16 show all the 48 countries in the background so that readers will know the relative positions of these six countries.

Both Figs. 3.13 and 3.14 indicate that the long-term NIC—human capital and renewal capital of this country cluster is still at the bottom left corner of the graph. That is, their long-term NIC competitiveness is weak among the 48 countries. The human capital of Argentina and Chile is higher than that of other countries; however, their renewal capital in 2010 is still lower than that of Brazil and Venezuela. For future sustainability, these two long-term oriented capitals deserve special attention.

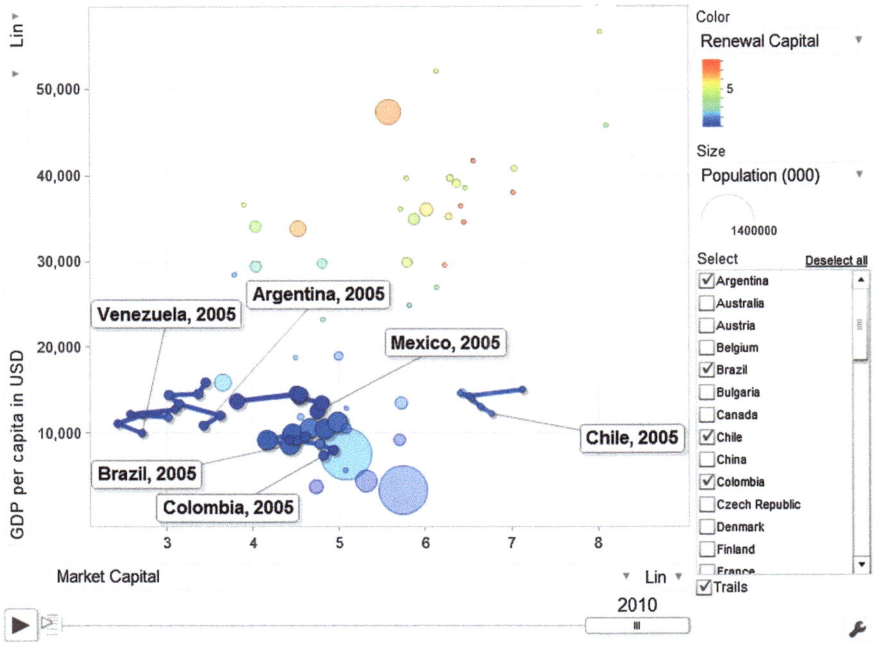

Fig. 3.10 The development of market capital and GDP per capita (ppp) for the six Latin American countries from 2005 to 2010

Figures 3.15 and 3.16 map market capital and process capital of the six countries on a coordinate. Market capital refers to the general assets embodied in a nation's relationship with international markets while process capital refers to the national infrastructure. For short-term competition, these are the two types of capital that can be expected to produce faster results if a nation is willing to engage in more extensive investments.

These two figures indicate the development of short-term NIC—market capital and process capital in three clusters: Chile leads; Brazil, Colombia, and Mexico together in the middle; and then Argentina and Venezuela lag behind. During the financial crisis, the short-term NIC of these six countries generally declined, however most of them rebounded in 2010, reflecting it is susceptible to external impact.

Dynamics of National Intellectual Capital in Three Time Periods

The previous illustrations and graphs describe more internal progression or regression of NIC in each country with individual capital score changes over the 6 years and the path of development of various capitals. The ranking changes to be

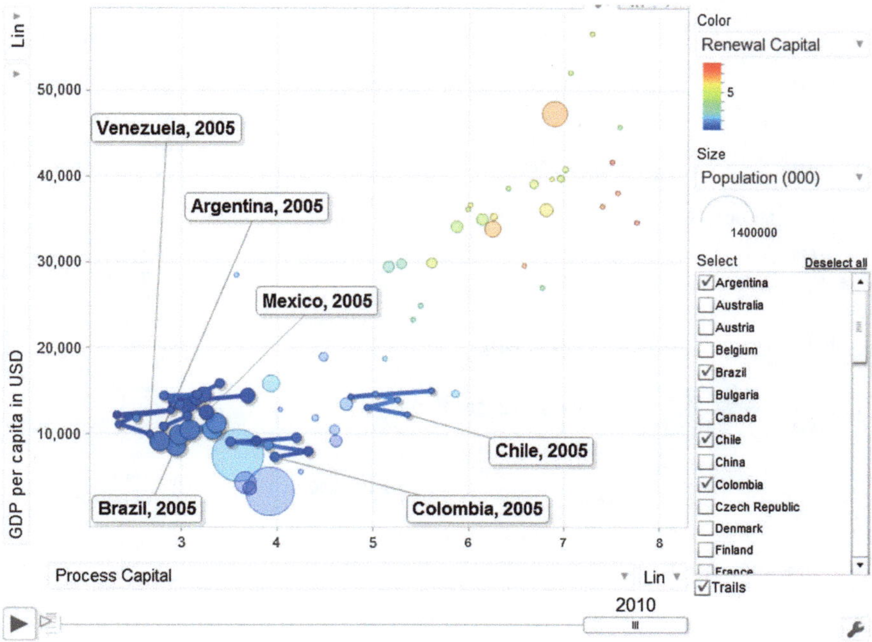

Fig. 3.11 The development of process capital and GDP per capita (ppp) for the six Latin American countries from 2005 to 2010

introduced in this section represent external competitiveness. Ranking, by and large, is a zero-sum game in which the advance of one country simultaneously marks the decline of another.

In order to probe the dynamics of NIC change before and after the financial crisis, we plotted Figs. 3.17, 3.18, 3.19, 3.20, 3.21, 3.22, 3.23, 3.24, 3.25, 3.26, 3.27, and 3.28 according to Table 3.2 in three time periods: 2005–2006, 2007–2008, and 2009–2010. To have a clearer presentation, we separate the data in two sets. The first set contains capital scores and ranking changes of human capital, market capital, and process capital in Figs. 3.17, 3.19, 3.21, 3.23, 3.25, and 3.27. The second set exhibits capital scores and ranking changes of renewal capital, financial capital, and average NIC in Figs. 3.18, 3.20, 3.22, 3.24, 3.26, and 3.28.

The figures are mapped based on the mean capital scores and ranking changes of each period. Ranking change in Figs. 3.17, 3.18, 3.19, 3.20, 3.21, 3.22, 3.23, 3.24, 3.25, 3.26, 3.27, and 3.28 is next to each capital score and copied from the bold-faced ranking difference of columns 2, 5, 7, and 9 of Table 3.2. Taking the human capital ranking difference of Argentina (4, 0, 4, 3) as example, the first ranking change "4" representing the difference between the 3rd (2009–2010) and 1st (2005–2006) period is plotted at 2005; ranking change "0" representing the difference between the 2nd period (2007–2008) and 1st (2005–2006) is plotted at 2007; another ranking change "4" representing the difference between the 3rd

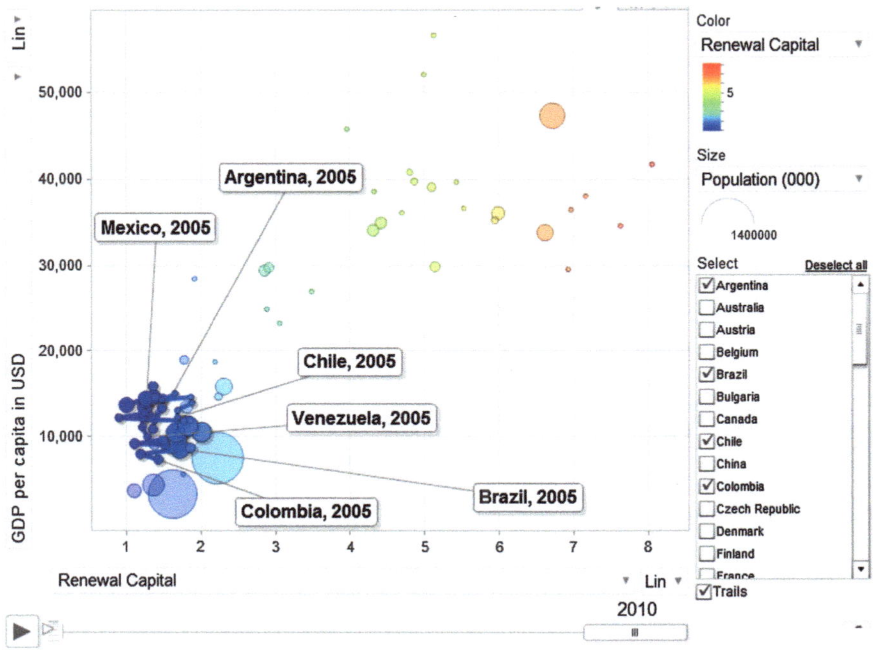

Fig. 3.12 The development of renewal capital and GDP per capita (ppp) for the six Latin American countries from 2005 to 2010

period (2009–2010) and 2nd (2007–2008) is plotted at 2009; and ranking change "3" representing the difference between the 3rd period (2009–2010) and six-years average ranking (exhibited in Table 3.1) is plotted at 2010. Special attention can be paid to the negative numbers, which means that the level of a particular capital was higher before than after the financial crisis. Since it is easier to read figures than tables, we will describe the finding of each figure separately.

From Fig. 3.17 and Table 3.2, it is apparent that Argentina's human capital increased after the financial crisis with relatively large-scale positive ranking changes (4, 0, 4, 3). In other words, Argentina advanced its international competitiveness in human capital after the financial crisis. The ranking changes of its market capital (0, 1, −1, 0) and process capital (−1, −1, 0, 1) with some negative numbers are in small scale.

From Fig. 3.18 and Table 3.2, the ranking changes of renewal capital (0, 0, 0, 2), financial capital (4, 3, 1, 2), and NIC (2, 0, 2, 2) indicate that Argentina gained international competitiveness after the financial crisis. Argentina is the only country in this cluster that has positive ranking changes in all types of capitals, comparing the rankings of the most recent (2009–2010) period with the six-years average. Overall, Argentina gained in NIC competitiveness internationally after the financial crisis.

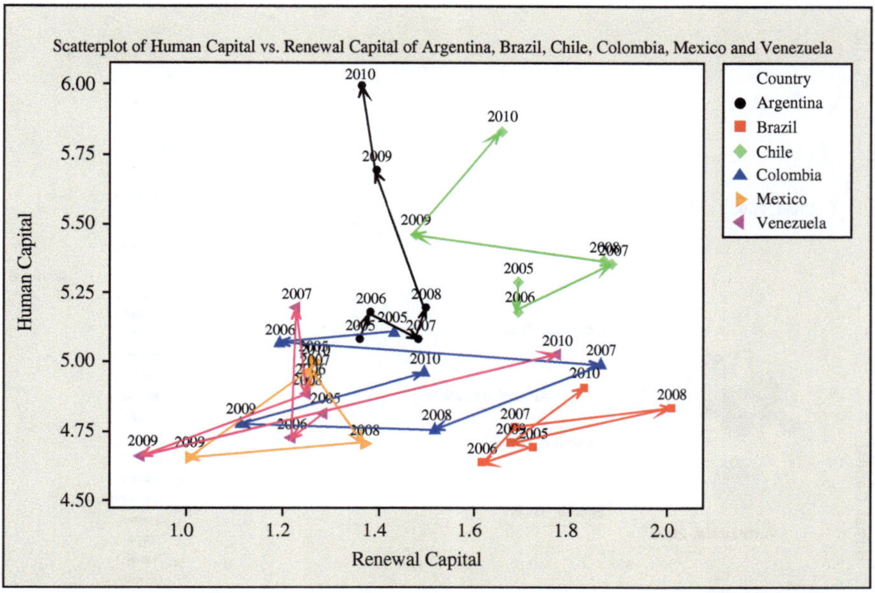

Fig. 3.13 Scatterplot of human capital versus renewal capital of Argentina, Brazil, Chile, Colombia, Mexico, and Venezuela

From Fig. 3.19 and Table 3.2, Brazil is particularly strong in its market capital with large-scale positive ranking changes (10, 7, 3, 6). That is, Brazil is gained international competitiveness in market capital after the financial crisis. The negative ranking changes of its human capital (−1, 2, −3, −1) and process capital (−1, 1, −2, −1) deserve attention.

Figure 3.20 and Table 3.2 show all positive ranking changes, meaning Brazil advanced its international competitiveness in renewal capital, financial capital, and NIC after the financial crisis. In particular, its relatively large-scale ranking gains in renewal capital (6, 2, 4, 3) indicate its promising renewal capability in future international competition. Overall, Brazil is the only country in this cluster that has such a large-scale ranking gains in market capital (6) and renewal capital (3), comparing the rankings of the most recent (2009–2010) period with the six-years average. Such findings agree with its good recovery after the financial crisis.

Figure 3.21 and Table 3.2 show that most of the ranking changes of Chile are positive, except one negative number in process capital. The ranking changes of its human capital (2, 1, 1, 1), market capital (3, 0, 3, 0), and process capital (2, 5, −3, 0) indicate that in general Chile is gaining international competitiveness in these three capitals in various periods. The ranking changes in process capital together with Fig. 3.3 explain that contrary to expectation, Chile's process capital ranking during the financial crisis was better than pre- and post-crisis levels. Specifically, it gained five ranks during the crisis, yet lost three ranks after the crisis. The last digit "0" in

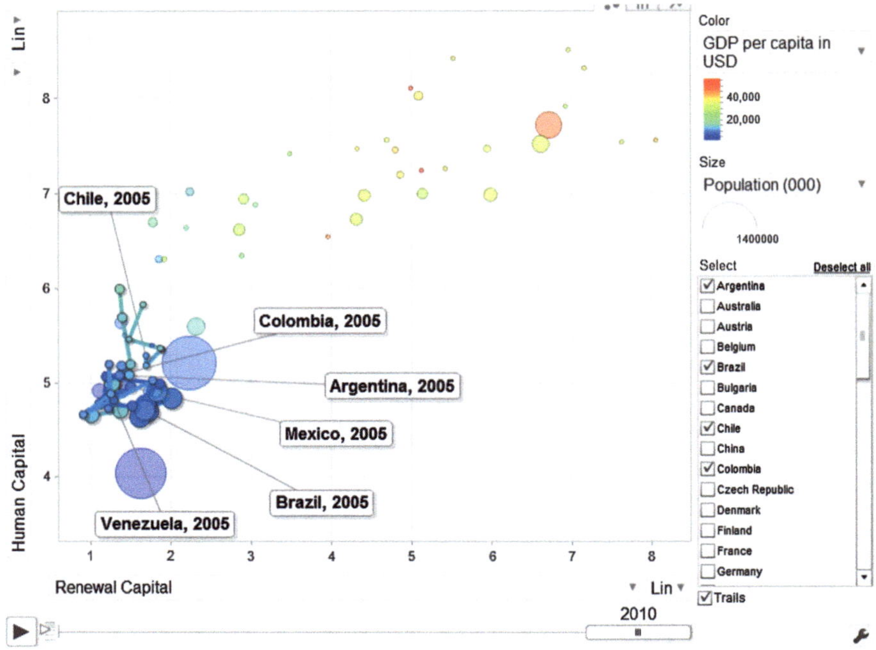

Fig. 3.14 Human capital versus renewal capital of Argentina, Brazil, Chile, Colombia, Mexico, and Venezuela

process capital means the ranking in the most recent period (2009–2010) is the same as that of the six-years average.

Figure 3.22 and Table 3.2 show that Chile had more negative ranking changes than positive ones in renewal capital (−3, 1, −4, −3), financial capital (−1, 0, −1, −1), and average NIC (1, 2, −1, −1). In particular, its renewal capital experienced a relatively large-scale ranking loss, with the last digit "−3" representing Chile's most recent (2009−2010) renewal capital is 3 ranks lower than its six-years average, a sign of losing international competitiveness.

Figure 3.23 and Table 3.2 show the ranking changes of human capital (−2, 0, −2, −1), market capital (−1, 1, −2, 0), and process capital (−4, −4, 0, −1) for Colombia. Most of the numbers are negative representing a loss of international competitiveness in these three capitals during different periods of the financial crisis. Especially, the decline of process capital international competitiveness is in a relatively large scale.

Figure 3.24 and Table 3.2 show that Colombia again had most of the ranking changes in negative number of renewal capital (−2, 5, −7, −2), financial capital (0, 1, −1, 0), and average NIC (−2, 1, −3, −1), ranging from 5 to −7. Ranking changes of renewal capital had the largest fluctuation. Contrary to expectation, Colombia had better renewal capital during the financial crisis than pre- and post-crisis, resulting in a gain of five ranks, yet it lost seven ranks afterward.

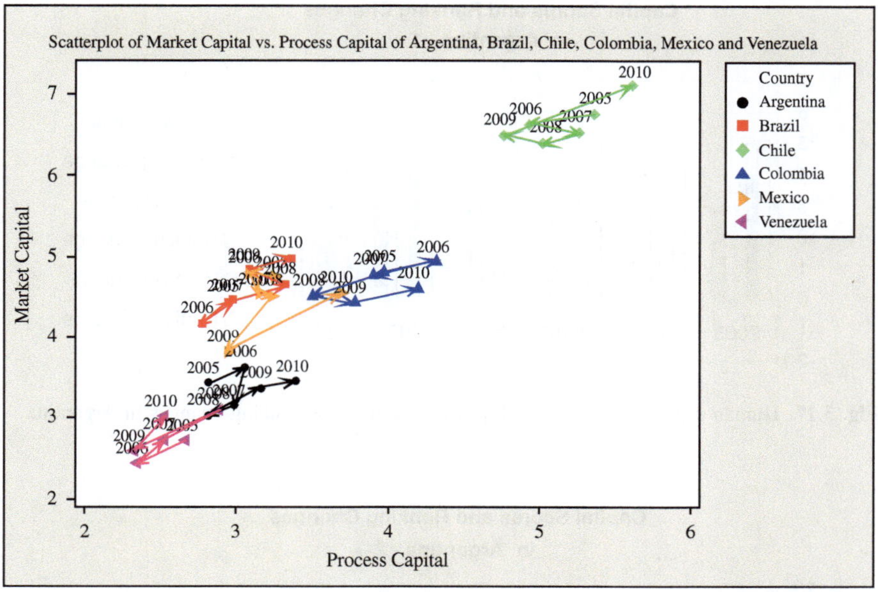

Fig. 3.15 Scatterplot of market capital versus process capital of Argentina, Brazil, Chile, Colombia, Mexico, and Venezuela

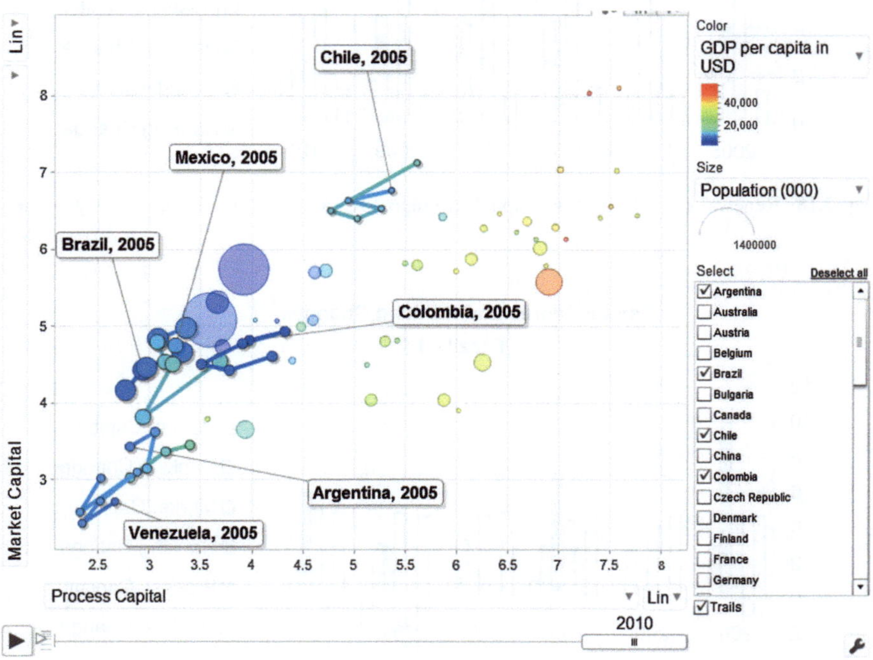

Fig. 3.16 Market capital versus process capital of Argentina, Brazil, Chile, Colombia, Mexico, and Venezuela

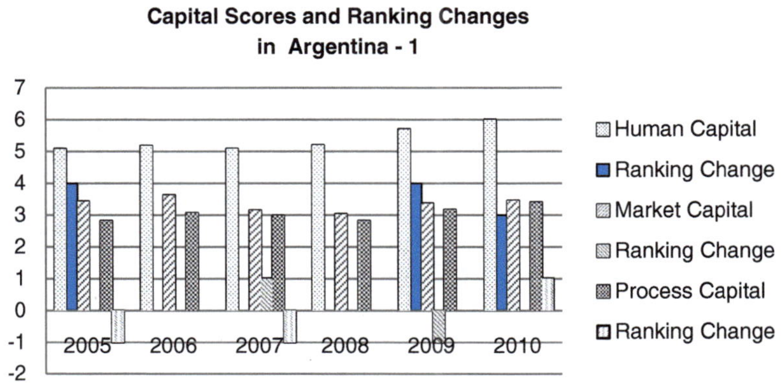

Fig. 3.17 Human capital, market capital, process capital, and ranking changes in Argentina

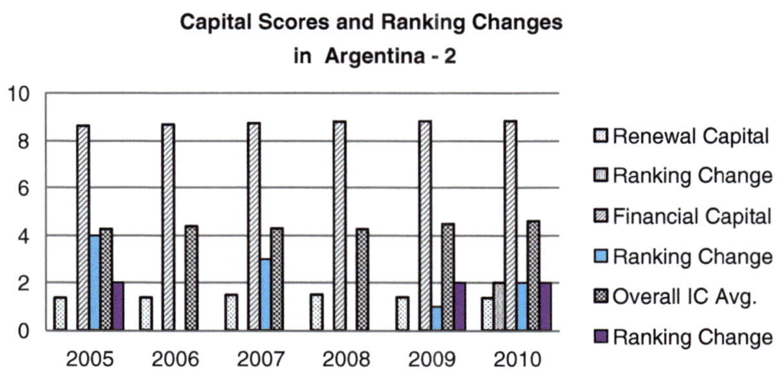

Fig. 3.18 Renewal capital, financial capital, average NIC, and ranking changes in Argentina

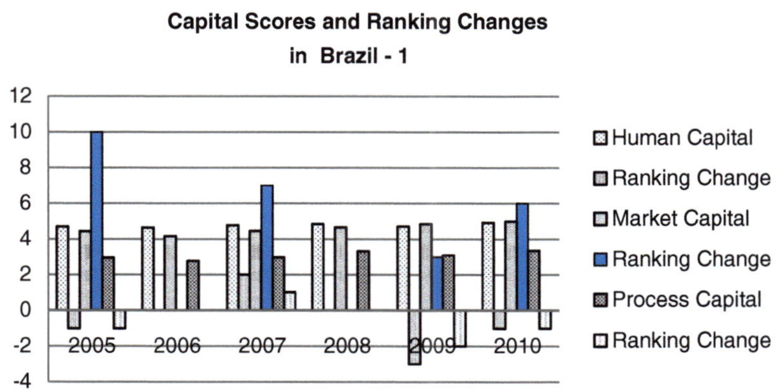

Fig. 3.19 Human capital, market capital, process capital, and ranking changes in Brazil

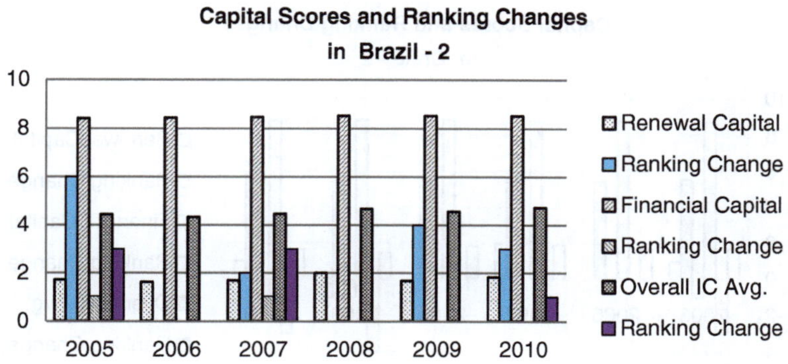

Fig. 3.20 Renewal capital, financial capital, average NIC, and ranking changes in Brazil

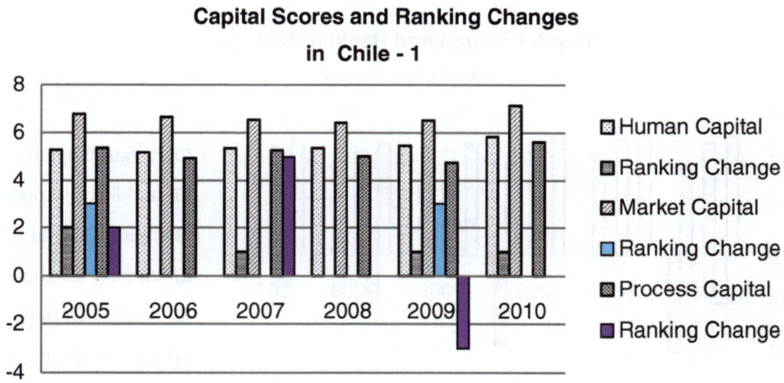

Fig. 3.21 Human capital, market capital, process capital, and ranking changes in Chile

Overall, Colombia is the only country in this cluster that lost international competiveness in all types of capitals (the last digit of all types of ranking changes are negative or zero), comparing the rankings of the most recent (2009–2010) period with the six-years average.

Figure 3.25 and Table 3.2 show that most of the ranking changes of human capital (−2, 0, −2, −1), market capital (−3, 1, −4, −2), and process capital (−2, −1, −1, 0) for Mexico are negative, representing losing international competitiveness. Especially noteworthy is Mexico's market capital became weaker after the financial crisis.

Figure 3.26 and Table 3.2 show that the ranking changes of Mexico's renewal capital (−1, 0, −1, 1) was minor. However, it had a relatively large scale ranking loss in financial capital (−4, 0, −4, −2) and average NIC (−4, 0, −4, −3). In general, Mexico has lost its international competitiveness in various types of NIC after the financial crisis.

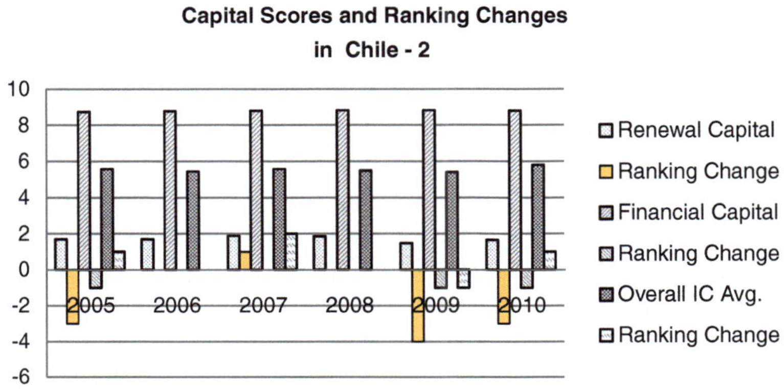

Fig. 3.22 Renewal capital, financial capital, average NIC, and ranking changes in Chile

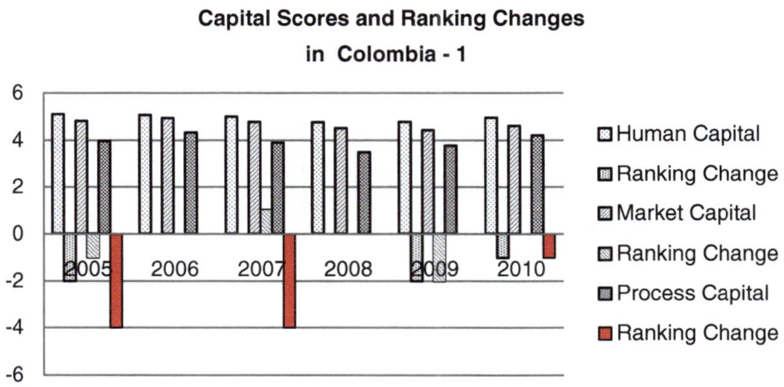

Fig. 3.23 Human capital, market capital, process capital, and ranking changes in Colombia

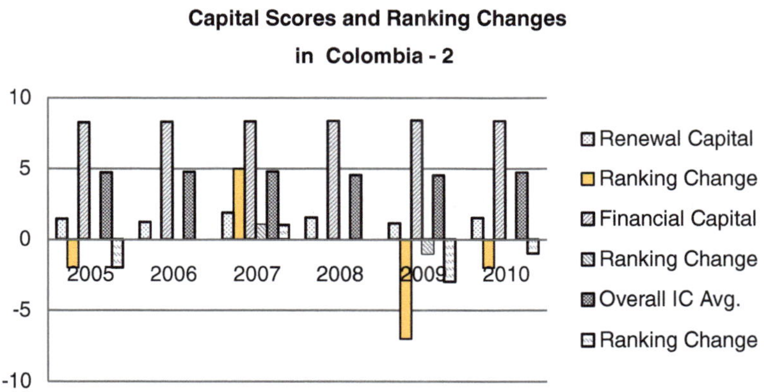

Fig. 3.24 Renewal capital, financial capital, average NIC, and ranking changes in Colombia

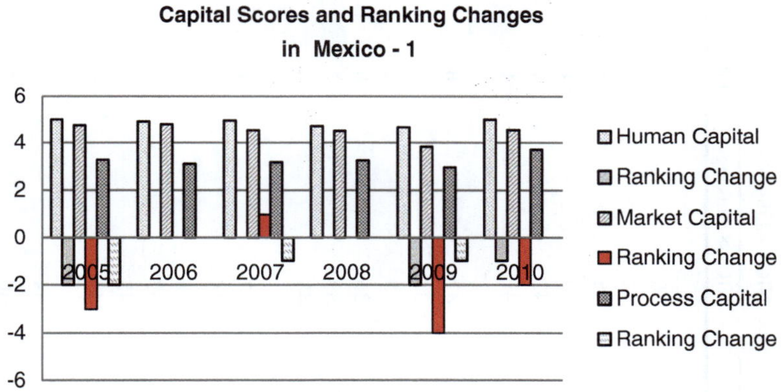

Fig. 3.25 Human capital, market capital, process capital, and ranking changes in Mexico

Figure 3.27 and Table 3.2 show the ranking changes of human capital (0, 4, −4, −1), market capital (0, 1, −1, 0), and process capital (0, 1, −1, 0) for Venezuela. Its relatively large-scale ranking changes is in human capital; however, the last digit of "−1" represents Venezuela's most recent human capital is only one rank lower than its six-years average.

Figure 3.28 and Table 3.2 show that Venezuela had good ranking gains in renewal capital (3, 1, 2, 1) and minor ranking changes in financial capital (−1, 0, −1, 0) and average NIC (0, 1, −1, 0). Overall, from the last digit ranking changes of all types of capital, Venezuela has relatively stable NIC international position. However, its market capital, process capital, renewal capital, and NIC are almost at the bottom ranking among 48 countries.

In summary, within this country cluster, Argentina gained its human capital international competitiveness after the financial crisis. Brazil gained its market capital and renewal capital international competitiveness after the financial crisis. On the contrary, Chile lost its renewal capital and Mexico lost its NIC international competitiveness after the financial crisis. Argentina is the only country that had positive ranking gains and Colombia is the only country that had negative ranking lost in all types of capital, comparing the most recent period (2009–2010) with the six-years average.

An important finding of this section is that internal improvement does not guarantee external international competitiveness. An example is Brazil's human capital. Comparing its average human capital of 2009–2010 and 2007–2008, there is 0.01 point improvement (4.81 vs. 4.80 in Fig. 3.1), yet it declined three ranks for the same period. Therefore, a country's internal improvement and external competitiveness need to be examined together to get a fuller picture of its relative position in the international arena.

Table 3.2 Ranking changes in three time periods for the six Latin American countries

	(1st period–3rd period)	1st period 2005–2006	2nd period 2007–2008		3rd period 2009–2010		3rd period ranking versus NIC ranking	
	Difference	Ranking	Ranking	Difference	Ranking	Difference	NIC 48 ranking	Difference
Human capital								
Argentina	**4**	37	37	**0**	33	**4**	36	**3**
Brazil	**−1**	44	42	**2**	45	**−3**	44	**−1**
Chile	**2**	36	35	**1**	34	**1**	35	**1**
Colombia	**−2**	39	39	**0**	41	**−2**	40	**−1**
Mexico	**−2**	41	41	**0**	43	**−2**	42	**−1**
Venezuela	**0**	42	38	**4**	42	**−4**	41	**−1**
Market capital								
Argentina	**0**	47	46	**1**	47	**−1**	47	**0**
Brazil	**10**	42	35	**7**	32	**3**	38	**6**
Chile	**3**	8	8	**0**	5	**3**	5	**0**
Colombia	**−1**	35	34	**1**	36	**−2**	36	**0**
Mexico	**−3**	38	37	**1**	41	**−4**	39	**−2**
Venezuela	**0**	48	47	**1**	48	**−1**	48	**0**
Process capital								
Argentina	**−1**	45	46	**−1**	46	**0**	47	**1**
Brazil	**−1**	46	45	**1**	47	**−2**	46	**−1**
Chile	**2**	30	25	**5**	28	**−3**	28	**0**
Colombia	**−4**	34	38	**−4**	38	**0**	37	**−1**
Mexico	**−2**	43	44	**−1**	45	**−1**	45	**0**
Venezuela	**0**	48	47	**1**	48	**−1**	48	**0**
Renewal capital								
Argentina	**0**	43	43	**0**	43	**0**	45	**2**
Brazil	**6**	39	37	**2**	33	**4**	36	**3**
Chile	**−3**	37	36	**1**	40	**−4**	37	**−3**

(continued)

Table 3.2 (continued)

	(1st period–3rd period) period2005–2006	1st 2nd period2007–2008		3rd period2009–2010		3rd period ranking versusNIC ranking		
Difference	Ranking	Ranking		Difference	Ranking	Difference	NIC 48 ranking	Difference
Colombia	**−2**	44	39	**5**	46	**−7**	44	**−2**
Mexico	**−1**	46	46	**0**	47	**−1**	48	**1**
Venezuela	**3**	48	47	**1**	45	**2**	46	**1**
Financial capital								
Argentina	**4**	36	33	**3**	32	**1**	34	**2**
Brazil	**1**	41	40	**1**	40	**0**	40	**0**
Chile	**−1**	32	32	**0**	33	**−1**	32	**−1**
Colombia	**0**	42	41	**1**	42	**−1**	42	**0**
Mexico	**−4**	31	31	**0**	35	**−4**	33	**−2**
Venezuela	**−1**	37	37	**0**	38	**−1**	38	**0**
NIC								
Argentina	**2**	45	45	**0**	43	**2**	45	**2**
Brazil	**3**	44	41	**3**	41	**0**	42	**1**
Chile	**1**	30	28	**2**	29	**−1**	30	**1**
Colombia	**−2**	40	39	**1**	42	**−3**	41	**−1**
Mexico	**−4**	42	42	**0**	46	**−4**	43	**−3**
Venezuela	**0**	48	47	**1**	48	**−1**	48	**0**

Remarks

The second column compares the 3rd (2009–2010) period ranking with the 1st (2005–2006)

The fifth column compares the 2nd (2007–2008) period ranking with the 1st (2005–2006)

The seventh column compares the 3rd (2009–2010) period ranking with the 2nd (2007–2008)

The last column compares the most current 3rd period ranking (2009–2010) with the original six-years average NIC48 ranking summarized in Table 3.1

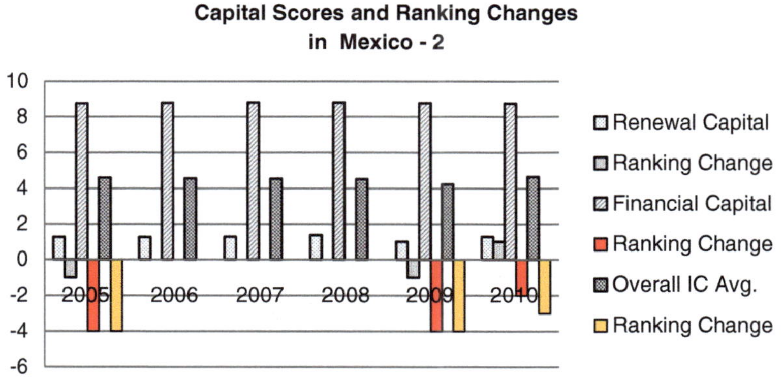

Fig. 3.26 Renewal capital, financial capital, average NIC, and ranking changes in Mexico

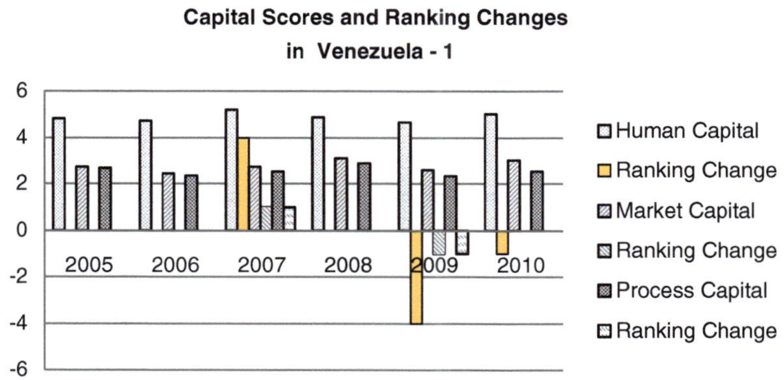

Fig. 3.27 Human capital, market capital, process capital, and ranking changes in Venezuela

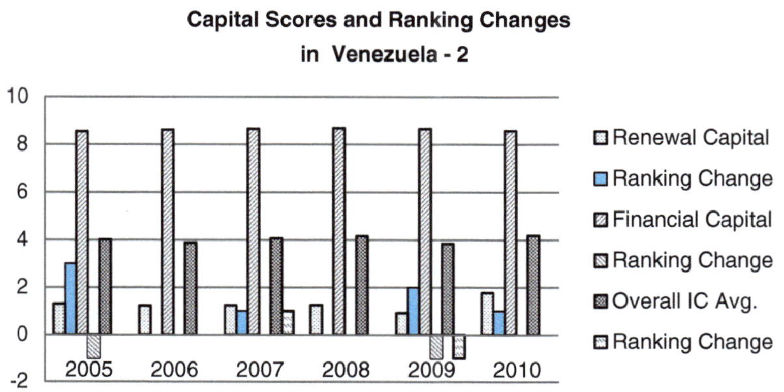

Fig. 3.28 Renewal capital, financial capital, average NIC, and ranking changes in Venezuela

3D National Intellectual Capital Trajectory

Up to this section, all the figures plotted different combinations of various capitals, capital–GDP codevelopment, and ranking changes on a flat plane. Even though Figs. 3.7, 3.8, 3.9, 3.10, 3.11 and 3.12 displayed four dimensions with color and bubble size as the 3rd and 4th dimension in addition to *X* axis and *Y* axis, graphically they are still on one plane. This section presents three-dimensional (3D) graphs showing each country's NIC development trajectory on a 48-country 3D landscape of various types. Since NIC evolution over time is always complex, combining different views from different angles may provide more comprehensive perspectives.

In what follows, we first explore the value driving context by uncovering influencing factors of GDP per capita (ppp) growth for Argentina, Brazil, Chile, Colombia, Mexico, and Venezuela from 2005 to 2010. Second, in explaining the GDP per capita (ppp) growth, we present the high, middle, and low capability which human capital, market capital, process capital, and renewal capital respectively have. Third, we examine the efficiency (GDP per capita (ppp) growth) enhancing factors and impeding factors of each country, taking each country's turning point into consideration. Last, we identify the efficiency drivers of each country in reaching a targeted GDP.

Figure 3.29 shows a rectangular 3D landscape, with a longer north–south side. The formation of the landscape is based on the data of 29 national intellectual capital indicators (presented in Appendix 3) for 48 countries covering six years (2005–2010), with a total of 8,352 (29 × 48 × 6) data points. In other words, Fig. 3.29 is the aggregated NIC landscape of the 48 countries. The relative NIC positions of Argentina, Brazil, Chile, Colombia, Mexico, and Venezuela (pointed out with arrows) are spreading from the middle to lower left side of the landscape. The enlarged trails indicate the NIC progression (upward), regression (downward) or changing configuration (sideward) of each country over the six years. Each white trail on the landscape represents a country. The altitude coloring from purple (north), dark blue, blue, green, yellow, and red (south) is computer generated, according to GDP values, with purple representing high GDP and descending to low GDP in red.

Figures 3.30, 3.31, and 3.32 are a set. Figure 3.30 presents four graphs indicating the high capability region of each human capital, market capital, process capital, and renewal capital in explaining the GDP per capita (ppp) growth. High capability means the data points are 20 % above the mean value of each capital. This figure shows that none of the human capital, market capital, process capital, and renewal capital of the six Latin American countries is in the high capability region.

Figure 3.31 displays another four graphs indicating the middle capability region of each human capital, market capital, process capital, and renewal capital in explaining the GDP per capita (ppp) growth. Middle capability means the data

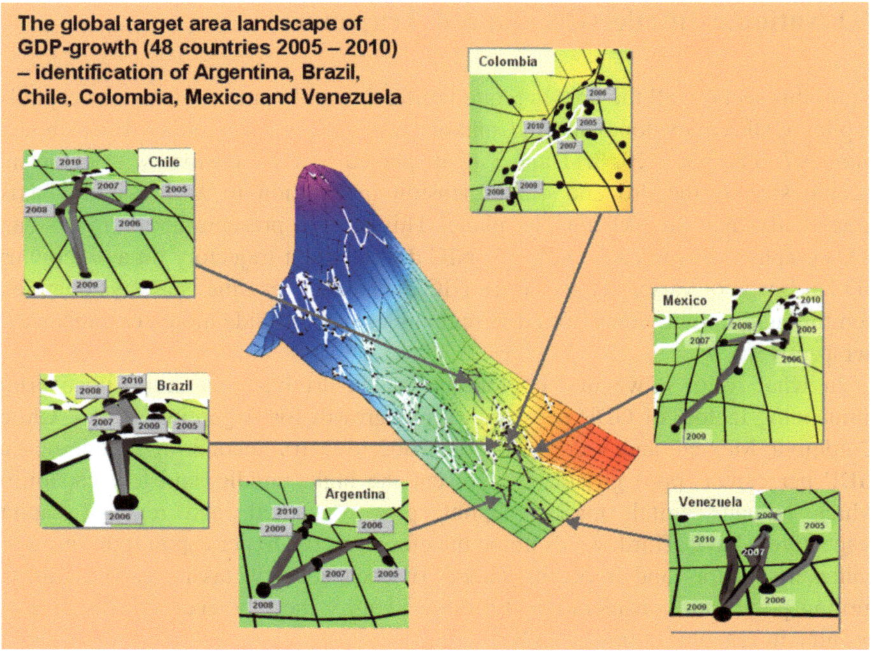

Fig. 3.29 The NIC trail of the six Latin American countries on a 3D 48-country landscape

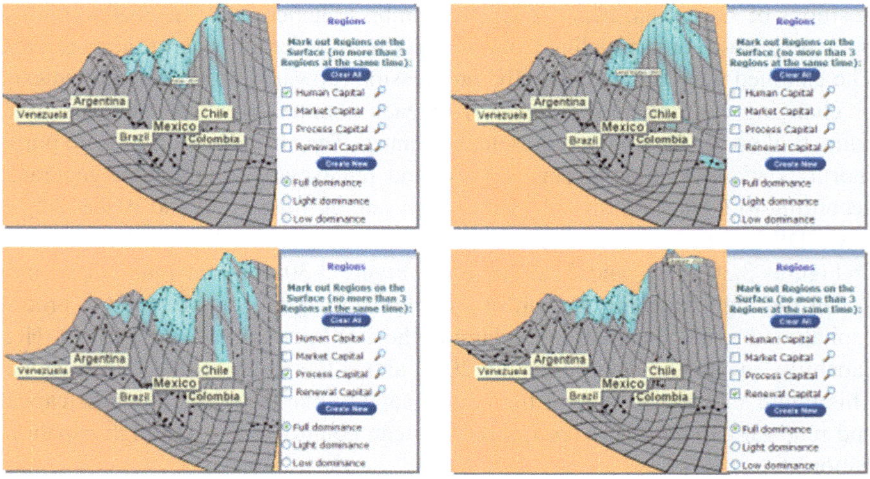

Fig. 3.30 The high capability region of human capital, market capital, process capital, and renewal capital with the relative position of Argentina, Brazil, Chile, Colombia, Mexico, and Venezuela

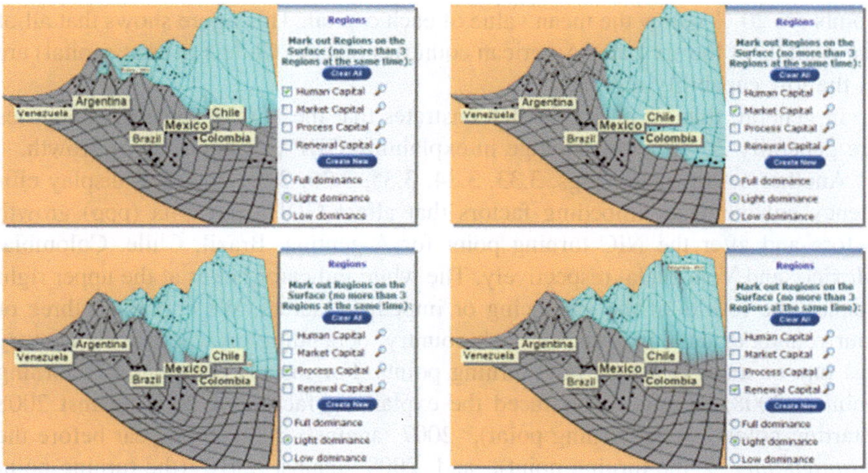

Fig. 3.31 The middle capability region of human capital, market capital, process capital, and renewal capital with the relative position of Argentina, Brazil, Chile, Colombia, Mexico, and Venezuela

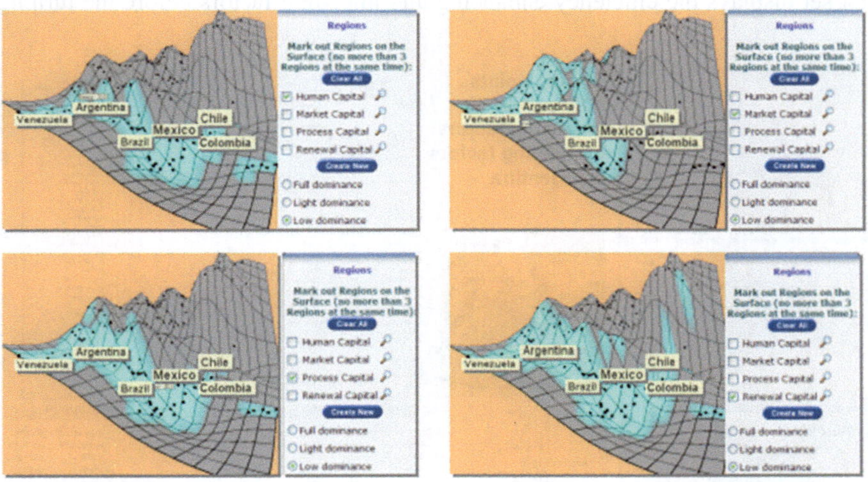

Fig. 3.32 The low capability region of human capital, market capital, process capital, and renewal capital with the relative position of Argentina, Brazil, Chile, Colombia, Mexico, and Venezuela

points are within the top 50 % value of each capital. This figure shows that only market capital of Chile is positioned at the middle capability region.

Figure 3.32 shows the last four graphs in this set indicating the low capability region of each human capital, market capital, process capital, and renewal capital in explaining the GDP per capita (ppp) growth. Low capability means the data points are 20 % below the mean value of each capital. This figure shows that all of the capitals of the six Latin American countries (except Chile's market capital) are in the low capability region.

In general, this set of graphs demonstrates that the NIC of these six countries are generally 20 % below average in explaining GDP per capita (ppp) growth.

Another set of figure, Figs. 3.33, 3.34, 3.35, 3.36, 3.37, and 3.38 display efficiency enhancing or impeding factors that affect GDP per capita (ppp) growth before and after the NIC turning point for Argentina, Brazil, Chile, Colombia, Mexico, and Venezuela, respectively. The white indicator boxes at the upper right display the results of the enhancing or impeding factors. We employed three or four rounds of data analysis for each country, depending on whether the country has one or more than one NIC turning points. For instance, Argentina's turning point is 2008; therefore, we traced the explaining factors of 2005 against 2008 (starting point $\rightarrow$ the turning point), 2007 against 2008 (one year before the *turningpoint* $\rightarrow$ the turning point), and 2008 against 2010 (the turning point $\rightarrow$ the ending point).

For an easy reference, we summarize in Table 3.3 two sets of results, each with the first five key factors. If there is a clear score cutting point (such as less than 1 % in the white indicator boxes), the reported factors may be less than five. The first set displays the efficiency enhancing and impeding factors before the turning

Fig. 3.33 Turning point and GDP per capita (ppp) growth enhancing and impeding factors of Argentina

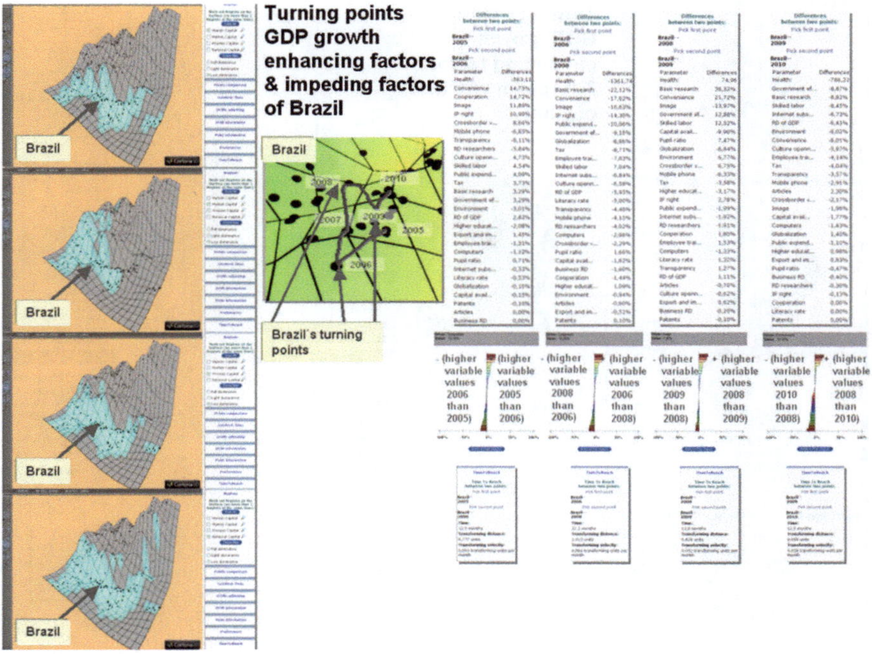

Fig. 3.34 Turning point and GDP per capita (ppp) growth enhancing and impeding factors of Brazil

point, the second set exhibits the efficiency enhancing and impeding indicators after the (last) turning point in italic letters. Since the factor strength (percentage) varies with different explaining power, we have calculated the average weight of the five enhancing and impeding factors and display each respective percentage in the rows for "Factor #5". We also count the frequency of four more frequently displayed categories, namely government-related issues (G), human capital related issues (H), market capital related issues (M), and research and development issues (R&D). Because capital availability was a concern during the financial crisis, we particularly highlighted this factor as "G-C".

Figure 3.33 shows the turning point (2008), the enhancing and impeding factors of Argentina. The four rectangular 3D graphs on the left-hand side of the figure indicate that all human capital, market capital, process capital, and renewal capital for Argentina fall into the low capability region (20 % below average).

From the frequency count summary of Argentina in Table 3.3, there are equal number of government (4) and market capital (2) related enhancing and impeding factors. For example, enhancing and impeding factor each has four counts of government related issues. All the four government related enhancing factors were surfaced after the turning point. In other words, all the four impeding government factors before the turning point were properly dealt with and turned into enhancing factors after the financial crisis. They are capital availability, transparency of

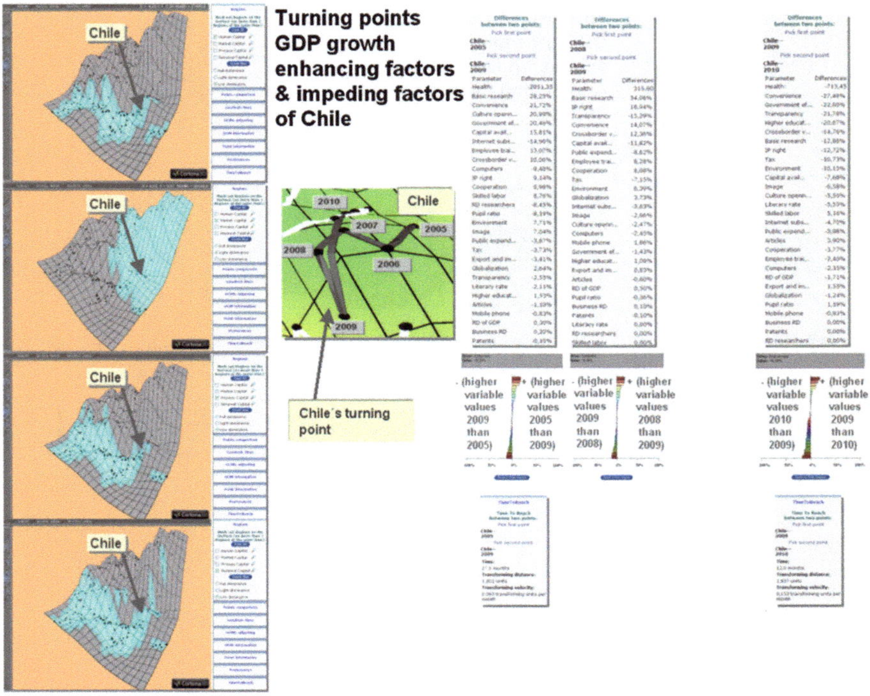

Fig. 3.35 Turning point and GDP per capita (ppp) growth enhancing and impeding factors of Chile

government policy, convenience of establishing new firms, and fair business competition environment. The two market capital enhancing factors are both cross border ventures, one before and one after the turning point. Image of country before and export of goods after the turning point are the two market capital impeding factors, reflecting Argentina's exports were negatively impacted after 2008.

In addition, employee training is an enhancer and there is no human capital related impeding factor, reflecting Argentina's best human capital (Fig. 3.1) among the six countries. The only R&D enhancing factor (basic research) before the turning point was turned to impeding factor after the turning point. Two other R&D impeding factors are university–enterprise cooperation and scientific articles, reflecting its low renewal capital.

For the strength (weight) of enhancing or impeding factors, Table 3.3 shows that before the turning point (2008) the weights of enhancing and impeding factors are similar 13.74 versus 15.11 %. However after the turning point, the weight of enhancing factors (12.27 %) was larger than the impeding factors (4.17 %), reflecting Argentina was doing relatively well during this financial crisis.

In Fig. 3.34, Brazil has three turning points—2006, 2008, and 2009. The four rectangular 3D graphs on the left-hand side indicate that all human capital, market

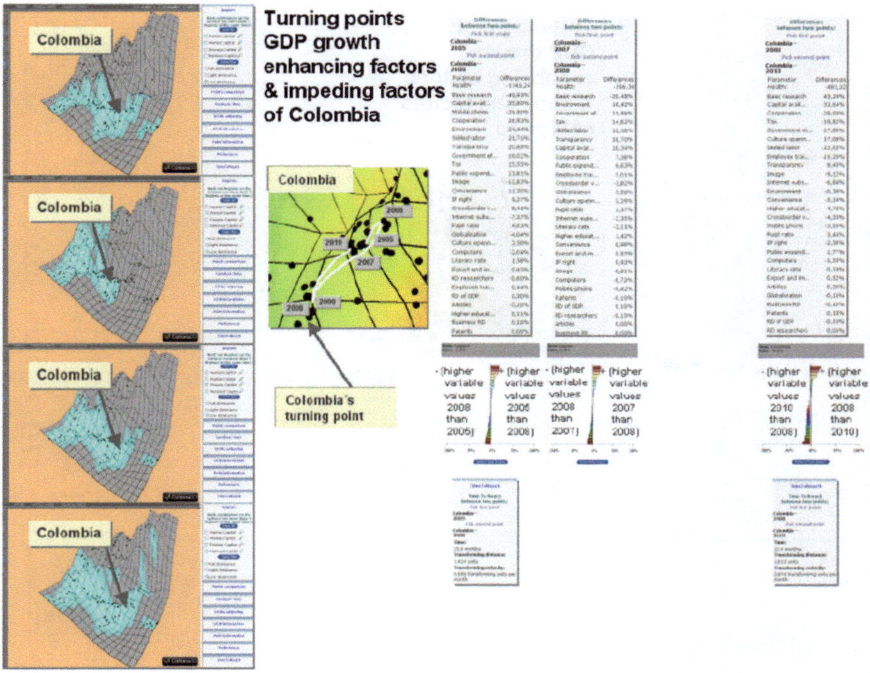

Fig. 3.36 Turning point and GDP per capita (ppp) growth enhancing and impeding factors of Colombia

capital, process capital, and renewal capital for Brazil fall into the low capability region (20 % below average). From the frequency count summary of Brazil in Table 3.3, there are more government related enhancing factors than impeding factors. The only government impeding factor is convenience of establishing new firms. For human capital related factors, higher education enrollment is an enhancer before the first turning point and skilled labor is also an enhancer after the last turning point. The major impeding factors include market capital and R&D related issues with three counts each. The average weight of 12.20 % before the 2006 turning point indicates that the five impeding factors, namely convenience of establishing new firms, university–enterprise cooperation, image of country, IP rights protection, and cross-border ventures deserve some attention. After the 2009 turning point, there are only two impeding factor with a very light average weight of 1.85 %. Interestingly, there is no market capital related enhancer even though market capital of Brazil improved after the financial crisis (Fig. 3.2).

Figure 3.35 shows that the turning point for Chile is 2009. The four rectangular 3D graphs on the left-hand side indicate that its market capital is positioned at the middle capability region (top 50 %) and all the others—human capital, process capital, and renewal capital fall into the low capability region (20 % below average). From the frequency count summary of Chile in Table 3.3, three each enhancing and impeding government related factors account for its GDP per capita

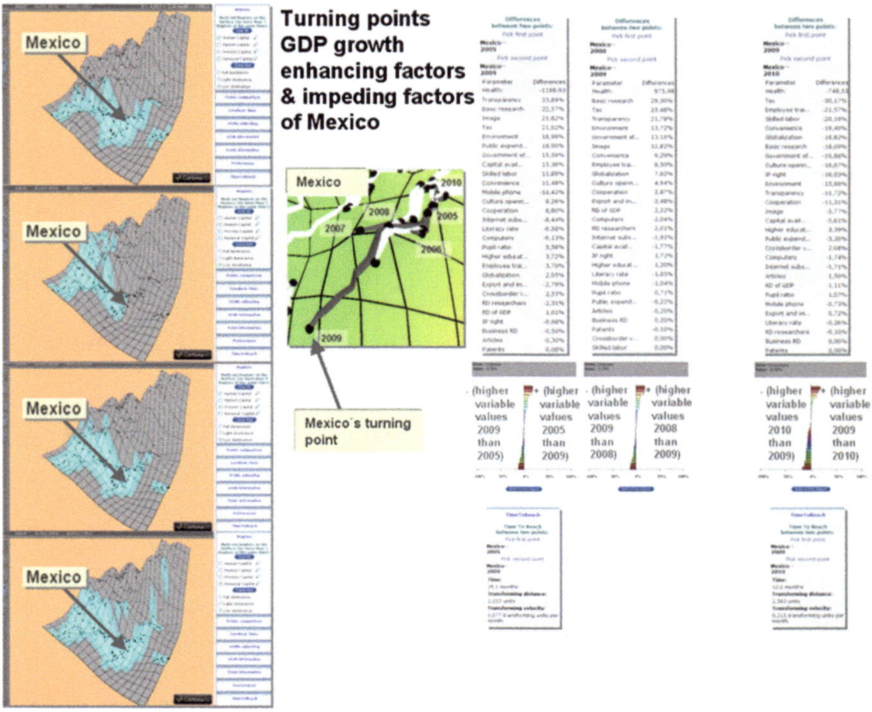

Fig. 3.37 Turning point and GDP per capita (ppp) growth enhancing and impeding factors of Mexico

(ppp). All the three government enhancing factors are present after the turning point. Two of them—convenience of establishing new firms and government efficiency are the transfer from impeding factors before the turning point to become enhancers, indicating improved public governance. The other government impeding factor is capital availability before the turning point, showing the financial stress during the financial crisis.

Chile has three enhancing and two impeding human capital factors. One of them, pupil–teacher ratio was turned from enhancing factor before the turning point to impeding factor after the turning point. Skilled labor is the other human capital impeding factor. The two market capital impeding factors include openness of culture before the turning point and export of goods after the turning point, also reflecting more needs for exports after the financial crisis.

For the strength (weight) of enhancing or impeding factors, Table 3.3 shows that before the turning point the weights of impeding factors is much higher than enhancing factors 21.45 versus 8.97 %, indicating the stress before 2009. However after the turning point, the weight of enhancing factors (21.50 %) was larger than the impeding factors (2.95 %), reflecting the relief after the financial crisis.

Figure 3.36 shows that the turning point for Colombia is 2008. The four rectangular 3D graphs on the left-hand side indicate that its human capital, market capital,

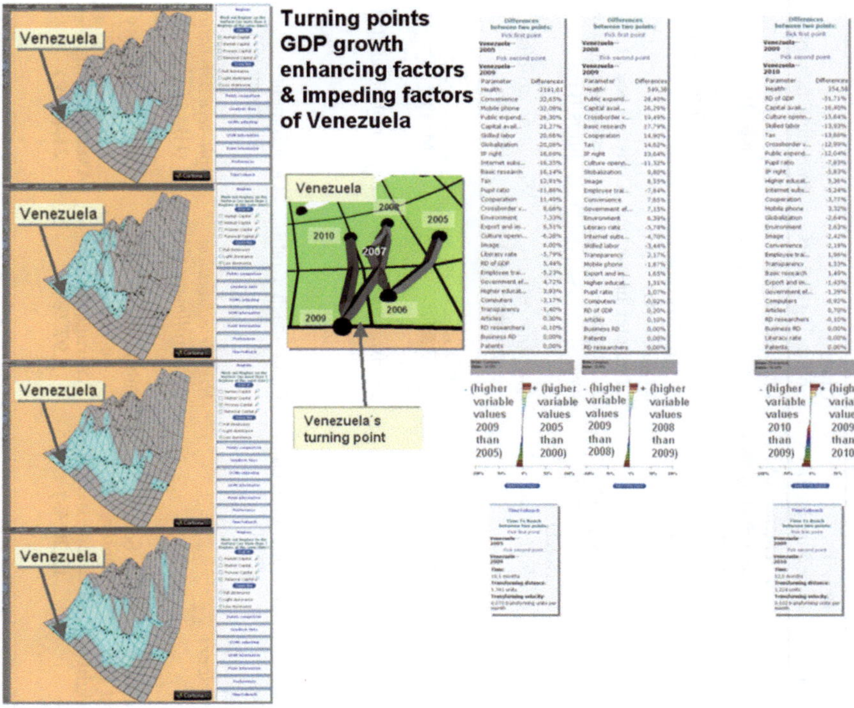

Fig. 3.38 Turning point and GDP per capita (ppp) growth enhancing and impeding factors of Venezuela

process capital, and renewal capital all fall into the low capability region (20 % below average). From the frequency count summary of Colombia in Table 3.3, there are more government impeding factors than enhancing factors (4 vs. 3). One of them—capital availability was turned from an impeding factor before the turning point to an enhancing factor after the 2008 turning point, indicating the effect of government stimulus. Transparency of government policy is consistently as an impeding factor before and after the turning point. The other government impeding factor before the turning point is fair business competition environment.

Colombia has three human capital impeding factors, one of them—skilled labor was turned from impeding factor before the turning point to enhancing factor after the turning point. The other two impeding factors are higher education enrollment and pupil-teacher ratio after the turning point. These results somewhat agree with Colombia's relative weak human capital, ranks 40 out of 48 countries (Table 3.1). The only market capital impeding factor is openness of culture after the turning point. In regard to the two each enhancing and impeding R&D factors, basic research was turned from enhancing factor before the turning point to impeding factor after the turning point; however, university–enterprise cooperation is the other way around.

For the strength (weight) of enhancing or impeding factors, Table 3.3 shows that before the turning point (2008) the weights of impeding factors are larger than the

Table 3.3 Enhancing factors and impeding factors of GDP per capita (ppp) growth for the six Latin American countries

Influencing factor	Argentina Enhancing factors	Argentina Impeding factors	Brazil Enhancing factors	Brazil Impeding factors	Chile Enhancing factors	Chile Impeding factors
Factor #1 before (1st) turning point	Mobile phone subscribers	Capital availability (G-C)	Mobile phone subscribers	Convenience of establishing new firms (G)	Internet subscribers	Basic research (R&D)
Factor #1 after (last) turning point	*Fair business competition environment* (G)	*Basic research* (R&D)	*Government efficiency* (G)	*Scientific articles (R&D)*	*Convenience of establishing new firms* (G)	*Skilled labor* (H)
Factor #2 before (1st) turning point	Internet subscribers	Transparency of government policy (G)	Transparency of government policy (G)	University–enterprise cooperation (R&D)	Computer in use per capita	Convenience of establishing new firms (G)
Factor #2 after (last) turning point	*Capital availability* (G-C)	*University-enterprise cooperation* (R&D)	*Basic research (R&D)*	*Globalization* (M)	*Government efficiency* (G)	*Scientific articles* (R&D)
Factor #3 before (1st) turning point	Employee training (H)	Convenience of establishing new firms (G)	R&D researchers (R&D)	Image of country (M)	R&D researchers (R&D)	Openness of culture (M)
Factor #3 after (last) turning point	*Cross-border ventures* (M)	*Scientific articles* (R&D)	*Skilled labor* (H)	–	*Transparency of government policy* (G)	*Export of goods* (M)
Factor #4 before (1st) turning point	Cross-border ventures (M)	Image of country (M)	Fair business competition environment (G)	IP rights protection (R&D)	Pupil–teacher ratio (H)	Government efficiency (G)
Factor #4 after (last) turning point	*Transparency of government policy* (G)	*Export of goods (M)*	*Internet subscribers*	–	*Higher education enrollment* (H)	*Pupil–teacher ratio* (H)
Factor #5 before (1st) turning point	Basic research (R&D) (**Average weight—13.74 %**)#	Fair business competition environment (G) (**Average weight—15.11 %**)	Higher education enrollment (H) (**Average weight—4.78 %**)#	Cross border ventures (M) (**Average weight—12.20 %**)	Public expenditure on education (H) (**Average weight—8.97 %**)	Capital availability (G-C) (**Average weight—21.45 %**)

(continued)

Table 3.3 (continued)

Influencing factor	Argentina Enhancing factors	Argentina Impeding factors	Brazil Enhancing factors	Brazil Impeding factors	Chile Enhancing factors	Chile Impeding factors
Factor #5 after (last) turning point	*Convenience of establishing new firms* (G) **(Average weight—12.27 %)**	– **(Average weight—4.17 %)**	*R&D % GDP* (R&D) **(Average weight—7.86 %)**	– **(Average weight—1.85 %)**	*Cross-border ventures* (M) **(Average weight—21.50 %)**	– **(Average weight—2.95 %)**
Category frequency count	G-4 H-1 M-2 R&D-1	G-4 H-0 M-2 R&D-3	G-3 H-2 M–0 R&D-3	G-1 H-0 M-3 R&D-3	G-3 H-3 M-1 R&D-1	G-3 H-2 M-2 R&D-2

Influencing factor	Colombia Enhancing factors	Colombia Impeding factors	Mexico Enhancing factors	Mexico Impeding factors	Venezuela Enhancing factors	Venezuela Impeding factors
Factor #1 before (1st) turning point	Basic research (R&D)	Capital availability (G-C)	Mobil phone subscribers	Transparency of government policy (G)	Globalization (M)	Convenience of establishing new firms (G)
Factor #1 after (last) turning point	*Capital availability* (G-C)	*Basic research* (R&D)	*Tax encouragement* (G)	*Higher education enrollment* (H)	*R&D % GDP* (R&D)	*Higher education enrollment* (H)
Factor #2 before (1st) turning point	Mobile phone subscribers	University–enterprise cooperation (R&D)	Internet subscribers	Basic research (R&D)	Mobile phone subscribers	Cross border ventures (M)
Factor #2 after (last) turning point	*University–enterprise cooperation* (R&D)	*Openness of culture* (M)	*Employee training* (H)	*Cross-border ventures* (M)	*Capital availability* (G-C)	*Mobile phone subscribers*
Factor #3 before (1st) turning point	Image of country (M)	Fair business competition environment (G)	Literacy rate (H)	Image of country (M)	Capital availability (G-C)	Fair business competition environment (G)

(continued)

Table 3.3 (continued)

Influencing factor	Colombia Enhancing factors	Colombia Impeding factors	Mexico Enhancing factors	Mexico Impeding factors	Venezuela Enhancing factors	Venezuela Impeding factors
Factor #3 after (last) turning point	*Tax encouragement* (G)	*Transparency of government policy* (G)	*Skilled labor* (H)	*Scientific articles* (R&D)	*Openness of culture* (M)	*Fair business competition environment* (G)
Factor #4 before (1st) turning point	Internet subscribers	Skilled labor (H)	Computer in use per capita	Tax encouragement (G)	Basic research (R&D)	Openness of culture (M)
Factor #4 after (last) turning point	*Government efficiency* (G)	*Higher education enrollment* (H)	*Convenience of establishing new firms* (G)	*Pupil–teacher ratio* (H)	*Skilled labor* (H)	*Employee training* (H)
Factor #5 before (1st) turning point	Globalization (M) (**Average weight—20.79 %**)	Transparency of government policy (G) (**Average weight—25.92 %**)	Export of goods (M) (**Average weight—7.07 %**)	Fair business competition environment (G) (**Average weight—23.78 %**)	Pupi–teacher ratio (H) (**Average weight—7.44 %**)	Public expenditure on education (H) (**Average weight—17.30 %**)
Factor #5 after (last) turning point	*Skilled labor* (H) (**Average weight — 22.78 %**)	*Pupil–teacher ratio* (H) (**Average weight—15.99 %**)	*Globalization* (M) (**Average weight—22.03 %**)	– (**Average weight—2.16 %**)	*Tax encouragement* (G) (**Average weight—22.31 %**)	*Transparency of government policy* (G) (**Average weight—2.96 %**)
Category frequency count	G-3 H-1 M-2 R&D-2	G- 4 H-3 M-1 R&D-2	G-2 H-3 M-2 R&D-0	G-3 H-2 M-2 R&D-2	G-3 H-2 M-2 R&D-2	G-4 H-3 M-2 R&D-0
Category frequency count—*Grand total*	G-18 H-12 M-9 R&D-9	G-19 H-10 M-12 R&D-12				

Remarks: (G & G-C)—government related issues including capital availability represented by G-C (total 37 counts including 7 counts of capital availability), (H)—human capital issues (22 counts), (M)—market capital issues (21 counts), (R&D)—research and development (21 counts)

enhancing factors, 25.92 versus 20.79 %. However after the turning point, the weight of enhancing factors (22.78 %) was larger than the impeding factors (15.99 %).

Figure 3.37 shows that the turning point for Mexico is 2009. The four rectangular 3D graphs on the left-hand side indicate that its human capital, market capital, process capital, and renewal capital all fall into the low capability region (20 % below average). From the frequency count summary of Mexico in Table 3.3, there are more government impeding factors than enhancing factors (3 vs. 2). One of them—tax encouragement was changed from impeding factor before the turning point to enhancing factor after the 2009 turning point. The other two impeding factors are transparency of government policy and fair business competition environment before the turning point.

The two human capital impeding factors are higher education enrollment and pupil-teacher ratio after the turning point. Cross border ventures and image of country are the two market capital impeding factors. For Mexico, there is no R&D enhancing factor. However, basic research and scientific articles are the two impeding factors, reflecting its lowest renewal capital ranking among the 48 countries (48 out of 48 in Table 3.1).

For the strength (weight) of enhancing or impeding factors, Table 3.3 shows that before the turning point (2009) the weights of impeding factors are larger than enhancing factors, 23.78 versus 7.07 %. However after the turning point, the weight of enhancing factors (22.03 %) was larger than the impeding factors (2.16 %), reflecting less stress after the financial crisis.

Figure 3.38 shows that the turning point for Venezuela is 2009. The four rectangular 3D graphs on the left-hand side indicate that its human capital, market capital, process capital, and renewal capital all fall into the low capability region (20 % below average). From the frequency count summary of Venezuela in Table 3.3, there are more government impeding than enhancing factors (4 vs. 3). Capital availability was an enhancer both before and after the turning point, indicating capital was not a problem for this oil rich country. Fair business competition environment remained an impeding factor before and after the turning point. Convenience of establishing new firms and transparency of government policy were the other two government-related impeding factors.

The three human capital impeding factors include higher education enrollment, employee training, and public expenditure on education. The two market capital related impeding factors were cross border ventures and openness of culture. For Venezuela, there was no R&D impeding factor.

For the strength (weight) of enhancing or impeding factors, Table 3.3 shows that before the turning point (2009) the weights of impeding factors are larger than enhancing factors, 17.30 versus 7.44 %. However after the turning point, the weight of enhancing factors (22.31 %) was larger than the impeding factors (2.96 %), reflecting less stress after the financial crisis.

To summarize Table 3.3 into an overall suggestion, we count the frequency of both enhancing and impeding factors by categories, shown in the last row of the table. Government-related issues (G & G-C) have a total of 37 counts, with 18 enhancing factors and 19 impeding factors. Since capital availability was a concern

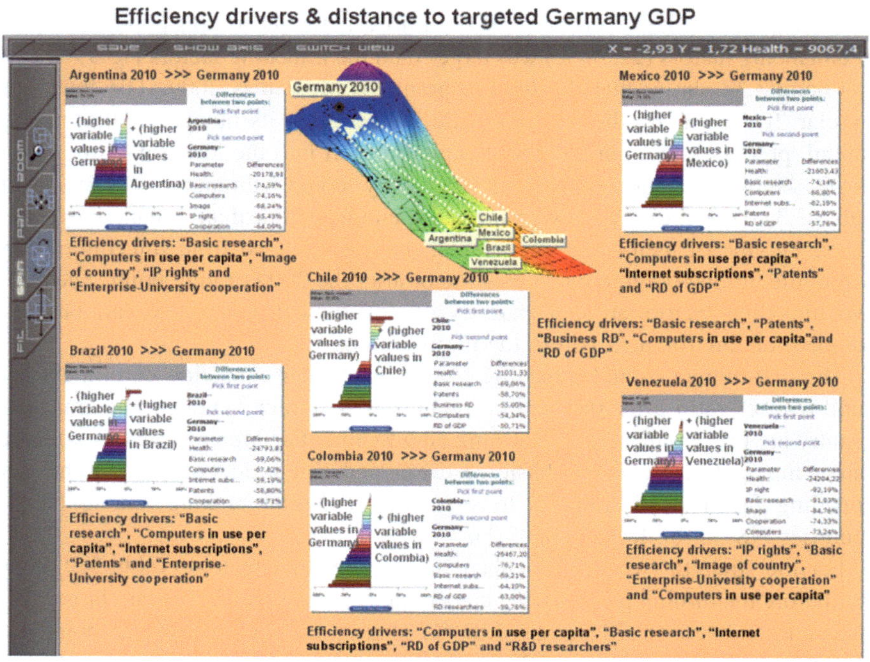

Fig. 3.39 Efficiency drivers and distance to targeted GDP per capita (ppp) of Germany

during the financial crisis, we particularly highlighted it by G-C. Out of the 37 counts, 7 counts are capital availability with two each for Argentina, Colombia, Venezuela, and one for Chile. For the first two countries, all their capital availability was turned from impeding factor before the turning point into enhancing factors after the turning point, reflecting the effect of government stimulus after the outbreak of the financial crisis. Venezuela's capital availability was an enhancing factor, both before and after the turning point, indicating its national wealth. Capital availability of Chile was the fifth impeding factor before the turning point.

Human capital (H) related issues have 22 counts, with 12 enhancing factors and 10 impeding factors. Market capital (M)-related issues have 21 counts, with 9 enhancing factors and 12 impeding factors. Research and development (R&D) related issues also have 21 counts, with 9 enhancing factors and 12 impeding factors, indicating the need for more R&D in these six Latin American countries. From Table 3.3, government-related issues turn out to have the greatest influence in achieving GDP per capita (ppp) growth. Overall, all these six countries have various combinations of mobile phone subscribers, internet subscribers, and computer in use per capita as their enhancing factors, indicating the needs of such basic infrastructure for supporting GDP growth. Table 3.3 provides a good guideline for each individual government to alleviate relevant impediments for facilitating future economic growth.

Figure 3.39 identifies the efficiency drivers (positive term) for each individual country. Efficiency targeting is akin to benchmarking. Efficiency represents GDP

Table 3.4 The first five efficiency drivers targeting GDP per capita (ppp) of Germany

Efficiency driver	Argentina	Brazil	Chile	Colombia	Mexico	Venezuela
Factor #1	Basic research	Basic research	Basic research	Computer in use per capita	Basic research	IP rights protection
Factor #2	Computer in use per capita	Computer in use per capita	Patents per capita	Basic research	Computer in use per capita	Basic research
Factor #3	Image of country	Internet subscribers	Business R&D spending	Internet subscribers	Internet subscribers	Image of country
Factor #4	IP rights protection	Patents per capita	Computer in use per capita	R&D % GDP	Patents per capita	University–enterprise cooperation
Factor #5	University–enterprise cooperation	University–enterprise cooperation	R&D % GDP	R&D researchers	R&D % GDP	Computer in use per capita
Average deficiency percentage of the above 5 drivers (%)	−69.3	−62.72	−57.56	−66.56	−63.94	−83.29

per capita (ppp) in this 3D software program. Since Germany stands out to be the most resilient country in the Euro zone financial turmoil, therefore it serves as a good benchmarking target for these six Latin American countries. In Fig. 3.39, the stacked small horizontal stripes are the deficiency factors of each country benchmarked against the GDP per capita (ppp) of Germany in 2010. The length of the stripes represents the degree of deficiency. For easier comparison, we list the first five deficiency factors of each country in Table 3.4.

With Germany being used as a benchmarking country, irrespective to the sequence of deficiency, the common areas that these six countries need to improve include basic research (six counts), computer in use per capita (six counts), internet subscribers (three counts), university–enterprise cooperation (three counts), R&D % GDP (three counts), patents per capita (three counts), IP rights protection (two counts), and image of country (two counts). That is, the areas that need improvement are quite similar for these six countries. Among the above eight common indicators, five (basic research, university–enterprise cooperation, R&D % GDP, patents per capita, and IP rights protection) are R&D related. These results agree with the very low renewal capital presented in Fig. 3.4.

Based on the average deficiency (negative term) percentage reported in Table 3.4, Venezuela has the longest distance (−83.29 %) to achieve the target GDP (Germany's), followed by Argentina (−69.30 %), Colombia (−66.56 %), Mexico (−63.94 %), Brazil (−62.72 %), and Chile (−57.56 %).

The added value of the above 3D trajectory analysis is to (1) display the NIC trails of the discussed countries on a 48-country landscape; (2) locate the capability region of the four individual capitals for each country; (3) highlight NIC turning points, details of the enhancing or impeding factors, and the dynamics of factor changes for each country; and (4) calculate the distance that each country has to progress in order to achieve the benchmark GDP and identify the first five key factors to reach this goal. This section supplements the previous sections by looking into the contribution of each individual indicator in each year, rather than average scores and average rankings.

In this chapter, we reported our research findings in layman terms with graphs and tables of various types for easier reading. This study on national intangible assets has uncovered some important findings that are not apparent in other GDP-related studies. For instance, the distance to the target GDP for Mexico (−63.94 %) is farther than that of Brazil (−62.72 %) even though Mexico has higher GDP per capita (ppp) than that of Brazil (US$13,790 vs. 9,982 for 2005–2010 average).

Chapter 4
Beyond the 2008 Global Financial Crisis

This chapter reports activities after 2010, commonly regarded as the aftermath of the 2008 global financial crisis (Kehoe 2010). Although some European countries were still in sovereign debt troubles after 2010, such as Greece requesting another bailout in early 2012 and Spain asking for external financial assistance in June 2012, we use 2010 as a cutoff point in order to be consistent with the reports of other country clusters in this booklet series. In what follows, we first introduce the general status of the Latin American region, information regarding multiple countries, and then the condition of each individual country.

Many factors have helped Latin America countries weather this financial storm, leading to a relatively good recovery. Financial crises are not new to Latin America. Past crises have prompted these countries to tighten financial regulations and launch structural reforms. During the past decade, such strategies have made the region more resilient to financial turmoil. Although still impacted by this financial shock, repercussions in this region were relatively fast, except Venezuela. However, the recovery varied by country based in part on policy differences, but also on exposure to the degree of reliance on the U.S. economy and dependence on commodity exports (Nanto 2009). After the recession, most central banks were ready and willing to let their exchange rates depreciate and serve as natural shock absorbers, except for Venezuela (Porzecanski 2009). Initially, investors were skeptical about the economic prospect of the region. By September 2009, both regional stock and currency indexes recovered 60 % of their losses, indicating renewed interest and confidence in Latin America's ability to rebound from the downturn and perhaps emerge from it ahead of many developed economies (Nanto 2009). The exceptions were Argentina and Venezuela, which share a heavy dependence on commodity exports and weak economic policy frameworks (Nanto 2009). In general, relatively sound macroeconomic fundamentals and policy responses by many Latin American countries and international financial organizations have ameliorated what could have been a deeper and longer regional decline (Nanto 2009).

Around 1 year after the rebound, the global outlook worsened in the second quarter of 2011 as stimulus programs failed to achieve self-sustained growth in the developed world, leading to a downward revision of past economic data and future

C. Y.-Y. Lin et al., *National Intellectual Capital and the Financial Crisis in Argentina, Brazil, Chile, Colombia, Mexico, and Venezuela*, SpringerBriefs in Economics,
DOI: 10.1007/978-1-4614-8921-4_4, © The Author(s) 2014

growth prospects (Levy-Yeyati and Cohan 2011). Impacted by the combined effects of financial stress and dwindling global demand, Latin America also felt the pain of the rapidly deteriorating global context (Levy-Yeyati and Cohan 2011). As of early 2013, concerns about the fiscal and EU debt problems continued to weigh on the global economic outlook. Nevertheless, it is valuable to know what has happened to each country in the wake of the crisis.

Argentina

By the middle of 2010, the economy in Argentina had recovered from a sharp economic contraction in 2009 as a result of higher commodity prices (Heritage 2012a). The growth has been driven mainly by the agricultural sector and exports of agricultural commodities (England 2011). Argentina's economy grew 9.2 % during the last quarter of 2010 compared to the same period in 2009 (Del Pont 2011). The country's GDP also increased 2.5 % compared to the previous trimester (Del Pont 2011; Morales and Matthews 2011). Its soy exports rose to nearly US$20 billion representing more than a quarter of total export earnings (Morales and Matthews 2011). The auto industry has driven surging factory output, as car production rose 41 % in 2010 (Morales and Matthews 2011). Private consumption increase of 11.5 % during the last quarter of 2010, public spending increase of 30 % in 2010, high exports to neighboring Brazil, and bumper crops all fuelled Argentina's strong performance (Del Pont 2011; Morales and Matthews 2011). Private consumption continued to grow in 2011 with investments rising to 24 % of its GDP, the highest percentage in the last 30 years (Del Pont 2011).

Argentina achieved a real GDP growth of 9.2 % in 2010 and 8.9 % in 2011 (Global Finance 2012a), the fastest in Latin America (England 2011). By many measures, Argentina is booming (The New York Times 2012) due to the following two factors (England 2011). First, its resource-based economy has benefited hugely from high commodity prices, with soy prices tripling since 2002. The country is now the world's largest exporter of soybean oil, and the third largest exporter of soy beans. Second, it has been helped by the growing economies of its two main export partners: China and Brazil. China is the destination for 90 % of the Argentine soya crop and is set to invest US$1.5 billion in agricultural sector infrastructure in Argentina over the next 10 years (England 2011). Brazilian growth, meanwhile, has underpinned demand for Argentine cars and manufactured goods (England 2011).

Argentina rebounded from its previous economic crisis of 2001 with steady economic growth, disrupted only briefly by the global slowdown triggered by the financial crisis of 2008 (The New York Times 2012). In 2012, employment had reached record levels and the poverty rate had been cut by more than half since 2007. The country continues to benefit from heavy government spending, high commodity prices, and strong demand from China for its agricultural products (The New York Times 2012).

Although the strong consumption boom is very apparent in Argentina, the government's continued reliance on expansionary fiscal and monetary policies risks exacerbating already-high inflation (CIA 2012; Gutierrez 2011; Segura 2011). The weak point in this encouraging growth scenario is inflation, which erodes consumers' buying power and pushes up business costs (Del Pont 2011). Inflation in Argentina soared to over 20 % in 2011, second only to Venezuela's among major Latin American economies (The New York Times 2012).

The strength of Argentina's economic rebound may be held back by the government's ongoing expansionary fiscal and monetary policies (Heritage 2012a). For 2012 growth, critics lower the forecast to 4 % from 4.7 %, mainly caused by Argentine government exerted more control over company boards. In addition, private investment and private consumption were further underpinned by strong government expenditure on pensions and other transfers (Segura 2011).

Brazil

The Brazilian economy began to improve in the second quarter of 2009 (Mendonça 2010). In 2010, its real GDP grew by 7.5 % at its fastest pace in 24 years, largely driven by record low unemployment and a confident new middle class of free-spending consumers (Lopez and Cascione 2011). Consumer and investor confidence revived, boosted by an export recovery mainly from China (CIA 2012; Michener 2011). With credit cards and rising wages, new members of the middle class are buying cars in record numbers, eating out at restaurants and taking their first-ever foreign vacations (Lopez and Cascione 2011). Brazilian central bank said that the rising capital spending (21.8 % for all of 2010) indicates that businesses are confident in Brazil's economic outlook in the coming years (Lopez and Cascione 2011).

Brazil's strong growth and high interest rates make it an attractive destination for foreign investors. Large capital inflows in 2010 have contributed to the rapid appreciation of its currency—"real" and led the government to raise taxes on some foreign investments (CIA 2012). As investors forced up the real's value, the currency has appreciated by more than 35 % since 2005 (Michener 2011). As a result of the strong real, Brazil's manufacturing sector is getting hit on exports, which has put greater pressures on business, particularly the manufacturing and industrial sectors. Both of them have become less competitive locally and abroad. Another issue of concern was although the tax breaks and loose spending implemented during the crisis helped boost the economy, they also left inflation above 6 % in 2010 (Lopez and Cascione 2011). Therefore, controlling inflation becomes one of the most important matters for the Brazilian government in the wake of financial crisis.

After a strong rebound in 2010, the country's economy decelerated because of tighter monetary policy (through both interest rate hikes and macro prudential measures targeting consumer loans) and a more neutral fiscal policy (through slower growth in expenditures and a higher primary fiscal balance) (Levy-Yeyati and Cohan 2011). Although it was predicted that the robust domestic demand and investment would continue to drive the Brazilian economy in 2011, the domestic market is slowing down because of weaker external demand and market tightening in 2011. According to a Morgan Stanley report, external demand from Europe and the U.S. were still dropping. Furthermore, the withdrawal of policy accommodation and stimulus package in 2011 was partly responsible for slowing emerging market growth down. Moreover, most emerging market economies are willing to settle for lower growth rates rather than for a quick boost to growth that puts the health of fundamentals at risk (Pradhan 2012). In November 2011, OECD reported that tighter economic policy and weaker external demand have helped to cool the Brazilian economy from the rapid growth rates seen in 2010 with a prospect of suppressing inflation. However, inflationary pressures have not receded and credit growth was still buoyant with activity still expected to grow at below-trend rates over the next 2 years (OECD 2011).

Chile

IMF predicted that Chile would lead growth within the region in 2010. Indeed, the Chilean economy started to show signs of a rebound in the fourth quarter of 2009, with GDP increasing more than 5 % in 2010 (CIA 2012). Chile achieved this growth despite the magnitude 8.8 earthquake that struck the nation on February 27, 2010 with estimated total immediate losses close to 17 % of its GDP (CIA 2012; US State Department 2011). By 2011, the economy had recovered from the effects of the earthquake, and most of the damaged infrastructure was restored. Chile's government received high marks from economists and its citizens for its countercyclical spending in 2009 (financed largely from saved copper revenues) to offset the effects of the global economic crisis (US State Department 2011). The earthquake caused only a temporary disruption in Chile's economic activity (Woods 2010).

Chile was well-poised for recovery from the financial crisis. In 2007, its trade balance was US$23.6 billion with the current account registered a surplus of US$7.2 billion (4.4 % of GDP). In the last several decades, the Chilean financial system has developed remarkably. Financial assets rose from 50 % of its GDP during the 1980s to nearly 200 % in 2008 (Briones 2010). The nation benefited from a substantial record of sound macroeconomic policy, including a structural fiscal rule, current fiscal surpluses during recent years, low levels of public debt, and a positive net asset position by the public sector (Briones 2010). According to the 2009–2010 World Economic Forum Global Competitiveness Report, the Chilean banking industry ranked 4th (out of 133 countries) in terms of soundness (Briones 2010).

Chile has learned the lessons from the past and has built a resilient financial system. Following Chile's 1982 economic and banking collapse, a new General Banking Act was enacted in 1986. From then on, its banking sector dependence on external financing has been relatively low. Most external debt is long term and held by nonfinancial companies (Briones 2010; Gregorio 2008). With effective prudent supervision, its corporate sector is also well protected against exchange rate fluctuations (Gregorio 2008). The combination of outstanding macroeconomic fundamentals and a solid financial sector allowed the country to confront the current financial crisis in very good shape (Briones 2010). This time, monetary, and fiscal authorities both reacted promptly and in a coordinated fashion. The central bank aggressively reduced its interest rate, from 8.25 % in January 2009 to 0.5 % in July of the same year, at the same time the government implemented a large fiscal stimulus package. The majority of the measures implemented were focused on low-income households and small to medium-sized companies, regardless of the economic sector to which they belonged (Briones 2010).

Chile's forcasted economic growth of nearly 5 % in 2010 was believed to lead to recuperation within the region (Briones 2010). Chile indeed achieved more than 5 % growth in 2010 (CIA 2012), partly owing to the fast recovery of China. In 2010, China was Chile's largest export market, followed by Japan, the United States, Brazil, and the Netherlands (US State Department 2011). In addition to its demonstrated great resilience in coping with the global economic downturn and the February 2010 earthquake, Chile prepared for an external shock far better than either Britain or the United States (Hutchinson 2009).

However, following this period of robust economic expansion, the Chilean economy started to slow, reflecting the spillover effects of the Euro area sovereign debt crisis through lower confidence and tighter credit conditions (OECD 2012a). With growth of 5.9 % in 2011 (Global Finance 2012b), a moderate easing of growth to 4.5 % was expected in 2012 as domestic demand softened and international financial conditions remained volatile (OECD 2012a). While slower growth and social pressures for higher spending in education increased the budget deficit in 2012, its fiscal policy should help achieve a structural deficit of 1 % of its GDP in 2014 (OECD 2012a).

A great achievement for Chile is that the OECD invited Chile to become a full member in December 2009. After a 2-year period of compliance with organization mandates, in May 2010 Chile signed the OECD Convention, becoming the first South American country to join the OECD (CIA 2012).

Colombia

In Colombia, foreign-directed investment began to recover in 2010, notably in the oil sector (CIA 2012). To safeguard farmers from the aftermath of economic crisis, around US$130 million from its 2010 budget was allocated for the Rural Capitalization Incentive program (Reinoso 2010). Despite the economic slowdown in

2009, Colombia continues to maintain strong economic fundamentals, including macroeconomic stability and openness to global trade and finance (Heritage 2012c). However in late 2010, Colombia experienced its most severe flooding in decades, with damages estimated over US$6 billion (CIA 2012).

In spite of the global economic and financial crisis in 2008–2009, Colombia's economy has continued to grow in recent years. As an oil export nation, the Colombian economy was less affected by the crisis than many other economies (Garces 2011). In 2010, real GDP grew by 4.3 % (3.09 % per capita (ppp) based on the IMD database), showing a recovery stronger than some major world economies, but slower than those of comparable economies such as Argentina, Brazil, Chile, Mexico, and Peru (Garces 2011). Strong domestic investment and FDI inflows contributed substantially to an increase in gross fixed capital formation, which peaked in 2010 at an 11 % growth rate. FDI outflows emerged virtually unshaken from the crisis, peaking in 2010 at US$6.5 billion, a sixfold increase vis-à-vis 2007 (Garces 2011). Some companies took advantage of the crisis to invest at record low cost and thus expand abroad.

While Colombia's real GDP grew by 185 % from 2000 to 2010, FDI outflows increased 20-fold (Garces 2011). Enhanced investor confidence coupled with sound macroeconomic policy and a rich resource base contributed to a strong increase in real GDP that averaged 4.1 % annually in 2000–2010 (Garces 2011). In the same period, exports tripled, inward FDI stock more than sextupled and the financial sector more than doubled (as measured by assets). The Colombian stock exchange experienced a 14-fold increase in market capitalization and index growth during the 2000s. At the same time, the economy began commercial and financial integration with other regional economies, resulting large intra-regional capital flows and more proinvestment policy making (Garces 2011).

In the wake of the financial crisis, Colombian government has encouraged exporters to diversify their customer base beyond the United States and Venezuela, traditionally Colombia's largest trading partners. The Colombian government is also strengthening economic cooperation with Brazil, Peru, and other Latin American countries (Xinhua 2009). The SANTOS administration continues to pursue free trade agreements with Asian and South American partners and a trade accord with Canada went into effect in 2011. In addition, improved relations with Venezuela have eased worries about restrictions on bilateral trade (CIA 2012).

At the beginning of 2011, Standard & Poor's raised the sovereign rating of Colombia to investment grade, two levels behind Chile, and, along with those of Brazil, Mexico, Panama, and Peru, ahead of Argentina and Venezuela. By the second quarter of 2011, the other two rating agencies, Moody's and Fitch, also joined S&P in giving Colombia an investment grade rating (Garces 2011). With the development, Colombia has earned back investor confidence, attesting to the country's mix of liberal frameworks for trade and investment with rather conservative regulatory, macroeconomic (especially monetary), and financial sector practices. The favorable rating also constitutes a safeguard Colombia against political risk, while positioning its economy and corporate players prominently in the region (Garces 2011).

Mexico

Following a deep recession associated with a strong global downturn, Mexico is experiencing a robust recovery, with GDP growth of around 5 % in 2010 (higher than projected 3–4 %) and 4 % in 2011 (OECD 2011). Export growth is expected to slow after the rebound of 2010; however, its stronger domestic demand kept the recovery on track. Owing to past improvements in the macroeconomic policy framework and financial supervision, Mexico weathered the global recession of 2008–2009 without fiscal or financial crises—a major improvement compared its previous recession (OECD 2011). Its resilient financial system particularly assists the economy transit through the international financial turmoil. Such resilience mainly result from: first, government banking system had adequate levels of capital; second, banks have maintained high levels of capital adequacy despite the adverse conditions; third, leverage ratios were lower than those observed in advanced economies with total assets between 10 to 11 times equity; and fourth, banks continued to generate profits during the crisis (Sidaoui et al. 2010).

In addition to the strong financial sector, Mexican government's responses to the effects of the global financial crisis also helped the country weather the economic downturn and improve conditions in 2010 (Villarreal 2010). The government used a number of tools, including macroeconomic policies, targeted assistance to financial institutions, and interventions by Mexico's Central Bank to cut interest rates and maintain the country's liquidity (Villarreal 2010). In addition, Mexico secured a US$30 billion swap line from the U.S. Federal Reserve and an IMF Flexible Credit Line of US$47 billion (Villarreal 2010). Although Mexico eventually did not use the credit lines, the arrangements helped to improve confidence in the economy. In 2010, Mexican government implemented fiscal tightening measures including public expenditure cuts; higher taxes such as a permanent increase in the general VAT rate, permanent and temporary increases in excise taxes, temporary increases in income taxes; and limits on tax deferral mechanisms for corporate groups (Sidaoui et al. 2010).

The U.S. trade data show that Mexico's exports to the United States from January to June in 2010 were up 38.2 % and imports from the United States were up 30.0 % year-on-year (Villarreal 2010). Particularly, manufacturing exports increased 34 % year-on-year during the first 5 months of 2010, with much of the growth occurring in automotive exports (78 % increase). The government also took measures in the fiscal year 2010 budget by including substantive tax reforms to offset revenue losses from lower oil production (Villarreal 2010).

In the first two quarters of 2011, export-led growth continued boosting the Mexican economy as GDP grew by an average quarterly annualized rate of 3.5 %, exports by 11.2 % and industrial production by 4.1 % (manufacturing by 6.2 %). During this period, domestic demand accelerated, and private investment and consumption also continued healthy expansion (Levy-Yeyati and Cohan 2011).

The first half of 2011 was a continuation of the previous three quarters with GDP growth being supported by exports and by domestic demand, and a very favorable inflation and financial market environment (Levy-Yeyati and Cohan 2011). For the second half of 2011, economy slowed due to an expected decreased GDP and industrial production growth rate in the United States, the anticipated end of the fiscal stimulus package, and intensified financial and fiscal problems in the Euro zone (Levy-Yeyati and Cohan 2011).

After the financial crisis, several labor market indicators have improved in Mexico. However, employment creation in 2010 was not strong enough to make up for the jobs lost in 2009 (ILO 2010c; OECD 2011). Due to vulnerable public finances in most of the developed world, GDP growth was expected to slow to just over 3.5 % in 2012, and be close to 4 % in 2013 (OECD 2012b). In general, Mexican recovery still depends on an increase in external demand, especially the U.S. economic recovery.

Venezuela

From the beginning of the crisis, Venezuela decided to cut spending (as a percentage of the GDP), in contrast to the policies adopted by other countries of the region. In fact, the total primary real Treasury expenditure in 2009 was 15 % lower than in 2008 (Vera Azaf 2010). In retrospect, studies on Venezuelan case led to the conclusion that the economic policies adopted in reaction to the crisis not only failed to moderate the impacts, but also had the opposite result (Vera Azaf 2010). The result of the policy is economic contraction of 2.9 % with 25 % inflation—one of the highest in the world, and further devaluation of bolivar (Venezuelan currency) in January 2010 (Anees 2010). By 2010, GDP growth was still negative at −1.6 %. Venezuela and Haiti were the only two countries in Latin America that experienced a decline in GDP growth in 2010 (Rodriguez 2011). Net public debt rose from 14 % of its GDP in 2008 to around 28 % in 2010 (The Economist 2011).

Venezuela has been adopting the policy of fixed foreign exchange. In 2005, Venezuela pegged its currency bolívar at 2.15 to the dollar; however, the government tolerated a legal parallel market that kept the country supplied with hard currency at a higher rate (The Economist 2011). In May 2010, the government closed the "parallel" unofficial foreign exchange market and created the "Transaction System for Foreign Currency Denominated Securities" to replace it at a price of 5.3 bolívares per dollar—in an effort to stem inflation and slow the currency's depreciation (CIA 2012; The Economist 2011). In December 2010, Venezuela eliminated the dual exchange rate system and unified the exchange rate at 4.3 bolivars per US dollar (CIA 2012). In January 2011, the government announced the second devaluation of the bolivar within 12 months. In addition to economic problems, in the first half of 2010, Venezuela faced the prospect of lengthy nationwide blackouts when its main hydroelectric power plant, which provides more than 35 % of the country's electricity, nearly shutdown (CIA 2012).

In 2011, the Venezuelan economy received a strong fiscal and monetary stimulus, which translated into the recovery of growth and the persistence of high inflation. In the first quarter of 2011, Venezuela's economy grew by 4.5 and by 2.5 % in the second. In particular, the country's fiscal management during the first quarter of 2011 was marked by a significant increase in public expenditures, which were fundamentally due to the recovery of oil prices and the greater contribution of oil exports to fiscal income following the unification of official exchange rates (Levy-Yeyati and Cohan 2011). Moreover, the fiscal stimulus, along with an improvement in the release of dollars by the Commission for the Administration of Currency Exchange)—translating into the greater availability of imported goods—has helped private consumption to recover by 3.7 and 2.6 % in the first and second quarters of 2011, after 2 years of contraction (Levy-Yeyati and Cohan 2011). An oil boom—with an average price of $99.50 per barrel for the first 9 months of 2011 and a projected oil export income of more than US$80 billion—combined with the fact that 2011 is a pre-electoral year have generated an economic recovery, despite macroeconomic mismanagement and the existence of profound distortions in the economy (Levy-Yeyati and Cohan 2011). However, even in the presence of an overvalued exchange rate and price controls, inflation continues to accelerate, having reached 26.9 % in 2010 (Gupta 2011; Levy-Yeyati and Cohan 2011).

Among these six Latin American countries, Venezuela is the country that has recovered the slowest.

Chapter 5
Future Perspective and Policy Implications

In early 2013, more than 4 years have passed since the outbreak of 2008 global financial crisis. The world will be different after this unprecedented and swift global financial downturn. Radical changes are occurring in the global banking landscape, business models are being revised, the balance of power is shifting in the markets, and new rules are being negotiated—with certain parties taking a hard line (Doerig 2009). Although some countries in the European Union are still in deep financial troubles, it is time to reflect what had happened during the past few years and what can be learned from this crisis for future coping strategies.

Latin American countries reported in this booklet entered into the 2008 global financial crisis with better financial systems than a decade ago. In addition, from past experiences, relevant government agencies have been able to respond to the crisis in a timely and coordinated manner, leading to a faster recovery than many countries in other regions.

The economic crisis provides an ideal opportunity to examine the soundness of a nation's economic system and the effectiveness of national governance. Definitely, some countries will learn from the experience and emerge to be more resilient, some will continue their structural reforms to build their future strengths, and some will still be burdened by their chronic problems. In other words, after this financial crisis, there are prospects as well as challenges. In this chapter, we first present the prospects of these six countries, and then describe potential challenges they may face in the future. What we describe hereafter is mainly based upon the OECD economic survey report for those countries, supplemented with other relevant reports. The prospects and challenges are meant to provide points of thought or discussion, but are not an exhaustive list. This chapter finishes with some policy implications.

Prospects

Latin American economies started to speed up again at the end of 2012, with Brazil's recovery from a period of stagnation. The region's growth averaged around 3.2 % in 2012 after 4.3 % in 2011 and 6 % in 2010. Latin America will

C. Y.-Y. Lin et al., *National Intellectual Capital and the Financial Crisis in Argentina, Brazil, Chile, Colombia, Mexico, and Venezuela*, SpringerBriefs in Economics,
DOI: 10.1007/978-1-4614-8921-4_5,

approach its potential rate in 2013, remaining the world's second best performing region after Asia (Coutino, Fuentes and Leon 2012).

In the region, the past decade has witnessed a strengthening of banking systems and a deepening of financial intermediation from the lessons of prior banking crises. Most governments have taken steps to raise bank capital requirements, enhance regulatory standards, tighten controls over offshore operations, introduce deposit-insurance schemes, improve accounting and disclosure norms, and open up the banking industry to foreign ownership. Irrespective to whether foreign owned or domestically owned, Latin American banks tend to meet high liquidity standards and maintain relatively deep capital cushions. Moreover, the international commercial banks which loom large throughout Latin America, such as Britain's HSBC and Spain's BBVA and Santander, were not greatly exposed in Eastern and Central Europe—and have in fact reported healthy quarterly profits; thus, they have helped to anchor confidence and to maintain financial stability in Latin America (Porzecanski 2009).

Latin America's resilience, in contrast with Eastern Europe's financial vulnerability, is explained by the progress made by many governments in Latin America in the past decade. Their measures include reducing currency mismatches, allowing for more flexible exchange-rate regimes, enhancing the capitalization, funding and supervision of their banking systems, encouraging the development of local capital markets, and implementing sounder and more credible monetary and fiscal policies (Porzecanski 2009).

According to estimation, Latin America's working-age population is projected to expand steadily until it peaks in the 2040s, at around 470 million potential workers, a net increase of 85 million comparing to the number in 2007. This expansion offers Latin America a significant demographic dividend if its economies can grow sufficiently to generate enough high-productivity jobs for a large, young workforce—much of it in urban settings (Cadena et al. 2011). Therefore, for a sustained prosperity, Latin America must take full advantage of its cities' economic potential as the region is more urban than any other developing markets, with 80 % of its population living in cities, compared with about 50 % in China (Cadena et al. 2011). In what follows, the prospect of each country is briefly introduced.

Argentina

With Argentina's fast rebound after the 2008 global financial crisis, experts have suggested that "now is the time for reform because the economy is growing strongly" and the nation is well-placed to make big decisions for sustainable growth. However, whatever new measures are implemented, they must be enacted quickly to be successful (England 2011). The following characteristics may assist Argentina to become a more prosperous nation.

Argentine economic performance will still depend basically on domestic demand, particularly on consumption and investment. Thus, the importance of policies aimed at favoring public and private investment is very important, since they are crucial for job preservation and creation (CEI 2009). Revenues from export taxes have also enabled the government to increase its spending on social and welfare programs. Subsidies are an integral part of government policy and are implemented in the energy, transport, rural, agriculture, and some industrial sectors. Government spending (as a percentage of GDP) has risen by 6.9 % in the last 3 years (England 2011).

In Argentina, years of trade surplus (US$11.4 billion in the 12 months ending March 2011) have allowed the country to accrue substantial cash reserves. The reserves, combined with Argentina's isolation from global debt markets, helped shield the country from the 2008 financial crisis (England 2011). As predicted, grain prices will remain high and give the government resources to implement planned programs. The economy will grow 3.4 % in 2013 after an estimated 2.3 % in 2012 (Coutino et al. 2012).

Brazil

Despite the economic situations in advanced countries are still faltering and global economy has a prolonged slowdown, Brazil's 2011 elected President Rousseff pledged to make economic growth and poverty alleviation top priorities, thus projected good future prospects for Brazil. Export promotion is a main component in its plans to generate growth, taking care of reducing the vulnerability to international financial market fluctuations at the same time. To increase exports, the government is seeking access to foreign markets through trade negotiations and increased export promotion (TDS 2012). For instance, Brazil and Mexico are starting negotiations on a free trade agreement so that both countries can benefit from the transfer of technology as well as shared growth and new jobs (Bloomberg Business Week 2010). In addition, the EU is Brazil's biggest trading partner and this relationship is likely to grow further as the Brazilian economy expands.

Boosted by an export recovery, consumer and investor confidence revived and GDP growth returned to positive in Brazil in 2010. Its strong growth and high interest rates make Brazil an attractive destination for foreign investors. With the large capital inflows and the increasing taxes imposed on the foreign investments, Brazil can formulate long-term national development strategies and implement structural reform for future sustainability.

Other prospects include the growing middle class with increasing purchasing power and government's on-going large infrastructure projects. As a result, private consumption and domestic investment are likely to become the major sources of growth in the years ahead. Such development can somewhat detach the economy from the external negative influence. In addition, its re-industrialization strategy covering high investment in steel, petrochemicals, defense equipment, construction of its first atomic submarine, and continuous technology advancement will provide more job opportunities for years to come (Cárdenas 2008).

Furthermore, its “Bolsa Família” program created in 2003 is successful in reducing poverty, hunger, and improving social development. Since its creation, the program has expanded rapidly from 3.6 million families in 2003 to 11.1 million in 2008, or a total of 46 million people benefiting approximately a quarter of the population (ILO 2010b). Its promotion of school attendance, health, and nutrition has positive effect on Brazil’s social development as well. The attempt to break the cycle of intergenerational poverty by improving the well-being and skills of children so they can overcome the social and economic barriers faced by their parents is also laudable.

For infrastructure, Brazil’s hosting the major international athletic competitions every year until the 2016 Rio Olympics will prompt the government to invest in roads, airports, sports facilities, and others (TDS 2012). The recovery will strengthen in 2013, propelled by the acceleration in investment to complete the infrastructure for the 2014 World Cup and the fiscal and monetary stimulus measures in place (2012).

The above stated factors are only examples that may open new prospects for Brazil’s future social and economic development. With a dedicated government and proper resource allocation, Brazil’s advancing to developed countries is only a matter of time.

Chile

Chile has great prospects after the 2008 global financial crisis. It has emerged from the recession that resulted from the global economic downturn and the economic dislocation caused by the February 2010 earthquake (US State Department 2011). Its economic strength has been underpinned by substantial macroeconomic easing, a well-capitalized banking system, and absence of imbalances in the private sector (Woods 2010). With openness to global trade and investment firmly established, economic recovery has resumed at a steady pace. In addition, the earthquake caused only a transitory dip in Chile’s healthy economic growth. Its financial system remains stable, and prudent regulations allowed banks to withstand the global financial turmoil with little disruption (Heritage 2012b). Chile’s national well-being can be further enhanced from the prospects of their national governance, government system, banking system, trading openness, economic development goal, and service industry development described hereunder.

National Governance

Chile has a responsible and predictable fiscal policy which guarantees public sector solvency and smoothes the spending out of copper income. Monetary policy is conducted by an independent central bank which uses an inflation targeting regime supported by a floating exchange rate (Gregorio 2008). The Chilean financial market is governed by high-skilled agencies and appropriate prudential rules. Banking supervision is under the charge of a public autonomous institution and another independent organization—Superintendencia de Valores y Seguros—is the main regulatory body for the domestic financial market, supervising all activities and entities participating in the Chilean securities and insurance markets. It enforces compliance with all laws and regulations governing the financial market, and has the power to impose sanctions (Briones 2010). On the demand side, the pension funds represent the country's major institutional investors. Their combined financial assets (totaling 90 % of the country's GDP) account for half the stock of financial liabilities of the Chilean economy. Pension funds investments are ruled by risk criteria and are supervised by a third regulatory body (Briones 2010). In addition, both the government and the central bank have invested in building solid reputations in the past few years. The strict adherence to the fiscal rule and the presence of a truly independent central bank will create a more resilient economy for Chile.

Government System

Chilean government has been extremely transparent in announcing its special measures, their detailed justification, and cost. All relevant information, including press reports and documents detailing each proposal, is available through the Finance Ministry's website. This transparency orientation has been strengthened by the implementation of a national transparency law in June 2009. The law requires every public service to provide public information on their activities and data records (Briones 2010). Government policies implementation did not introduce distortions in specific economic sectors; rather, they have tended to be based on general principles rather than favoring specific industries or interest groups (Briones 2010). One salient feature of the Chilean policy-making process is the rapid national consensus. Taking the 2009 stimulus plan as an example, 15 days after the plan was announced it was legally and unanimously approved by the National Congress in the form of Law. Chilean Finance Minister acknowledged the support received from a number of economic analysts, but especially those from the political class (Briones 2010).

Banking System

The well-developed financial sector with the size of the domestic financial market around 200 % of the GDP has been a crucial element in Chile's economic growth (Briones 2010). Chile has a solid financial system, with competitive and well-capitalized banks, appropriately regulated and supervised, and adopting international Basel II proposals (Bleger 2011; Briones 2010; Gregorio 2008). Individual assessment of the debtors requires a detailed analysis focused on their repayment capabilities, taking into account, among other factors, collaterals, maturity, interest rates, currency denomination, and so on (Bleger 2011). The soundness of the Chilean financial system has been identified as one of the country's major current assets.

Trade Openness

Increasing trade openness allowing for the diversification of import and export markets has been Chile's policy (Gregorio 2008). Its approach to foreign direct investment (FDI) is codified in the country's foreign investment law, which gives foreign investors the same treatment as Chileans. Registration is simple and transparent, and foreign investors are guaranteed access to the official foreign exchange market to repatriate their profits and capital. Net FDI in Chile in 2010 was US$18.2 billion, up 43 % over 2009 (US State Department 2011). Chile enjoys the highest degree of economic freedom in the South and Central America/Caribbean region, supported by sound public finance management and strong protection of property rights (Heritage 2012b).

Economic Development Goal

Chile's goal is to become the first Latin American country to overcome under-development, defeat poverty, and achieve per capita income of the OECD average (US$26,000) by the end of this decade (Barton and Krell 2011).

Service Industry Development

To reduce the reliance on copper exports, during the last several years the Chilean government has made efforts to develop global services (off shoring) as a new source of exports (Briones 2010). The global services focus was appointed in 2004 by an Innovation Council, which is in charge of identifying and supporting new export clusters based on innovation to increase the proportion of domestically added value. In 2009, global service exports (mainly associated with the financial sector) have reached US$1 billion, around 2 % of total exports (Briones 2010).

Colombia

Colombia has future prospects with the following described characteristics, including pro-business reforms, reduced external public debt, healthy finance, the rise of Colombian MNEs, regional stock exchange, free trade agreement, and international aid.

Pro-Business Reforms

For Colombia, the 2000s were characterized by enhanced national security and reforms to the investment framework that have attracted unprecedented levels of inward FDI and facilitated the growth of small- and medium-sized enterprises (SMEs) (Garces 2011). Pro-business reforms in the oil and gas sectors and export-led growth have enhanced Colombia's investment climate (CIA 2012). A particular focus is placed on improving regulation and fostering a stronger private sector (Heritage 2012c).

Reduced External Public Debt

Before the financial crisis, Colombia reduced the participation of the external public debt, decreasing the risk of external financial shock. Presently close to 70 % of the total public debt is in pesos and 30 % is in foreign currency (Ministry of Finance and Public Credit 2009). After Brazil, Colombia is the country with the lowest private external debt as a proportion of GDP, implying lower entrepreneurial sector vulnerability to exchange rate variations and lower refinancing risks (Ministry of Finance and Public Credit 2009).

Healthy Finance

Colombia enjoys relatively healthy finance. Its current account deficit is completely covered by FDI with a rate from net FDI to current account deficit of 156 % (Ministry of Finance and Public Credit 2009).

The Rise of Colombian MNEs

Outward FDI from Colombia has increased considerably in the past decade, with its stock growing from US$3 billion in 2000 to US$23 billion in 2010 after major policy reforms and a return of investor confidence over the past decade. The rise of Colombian MNEs (primarily within Latin America), reflects Colombia's nascent structural transformation into a knowledge-based economy and cross-border investment in services (Garces 2011; Ministry of Finance and Public Credit 2009). In 2005, procedures and transaction costs for domestic merge and acquisitions improved, so Colombia's largest MNEs were able to capitalize on domestic expansion through innumerable local acquisitions that positioned many of the top firms on a path of further growth (Garces 2011). The improved security situation, a stronger financial sector with increasing capital available for local MNEs, a combination of liberalized policy in trade and investment, and conservative monetary policy, and financial regulations have all contributed to strengthening

Colombia's economy and enabling the internationalization of its corporation (Garces 2011).

Regional Stock Exchange

In 2010, Chile, Colombia and Peru signed a commitment to create the first regionally integrated stock exchange, the Mercado Integrado Latinoamericano (MILA), which started trading operations on May 31, 2011 (Garces 2011). The MILA economies constitute the market in Latin America with the highest prospects for real GDP growth, estimated at 4–6 % per annum according to the World Bank. It will have the region's most diversified turnover as well, with growing exports to Asia, Europe and the United States.

Free Trade Agreement

The far-reaching free trade agreement between the EFTA States (The European Free Trade Association with members of Liechtenstein, Iceland, Norway, and Switzerland) and Colombia provides for easier access to markets for goods and services and includes provision in investment and in intellectual property rights, public procurement, and competition. This gives Colombia an opportunity to become more competitive and more attractive to EFTA investors. As part of the free trade agreement, Colombia will also receive support measures and technical assistance (SECO 2009).

International Aid

Colombia received various international aids that help its national development. The World Bank's Country Partnership Strategy (CPS) for Colombia covers poverty reduction, equality of opportunity, peace, balanced and sustainable growth, environmental and resource management, and enhancing government efficiency and effectiveness. Inter-American Development Bank approved in 2007 a loan of US$774 million, focusing on strengthening Colombia's competitiveness, in particular through SME support, improving business environment and infrastructure financing; promoting social development; and reinforcing public-sector institutions governance (SECO 2009). In addition, Colombia is a priority country for Switzerland's humanitarian aid, amounting to Swiss franc 8 million in 2008 and aiming at emergency assistance, reconstruction, prevention and preparedness, and advocacy (SECO 2009). The 2010–2012 program for Colombia (2010–2012) planned by the Swiss Agency for Development and Cooperation has helped improve Colombia's ecological efficiency. At the same time, Colombia is thereby enabled to avail of technology transfer and to participate in global emissions trading (SECO 2009).

Mexico

Mexico's future prospects may be enhanced with the following characteristics in the areas of government, financial system, fiscal policy, employment, free trade agreements, and technology cluster.

Government

Mexico had reformed its macroeconomic policy framework and had therefore strengthened its fundamentals. For instance, prudent fiscal policy management had helped to eliminate the large and persistent budget deficit, thereby contributing to a significant reduction in the public debt to GDP ratio (Sidaoui, Ramos-Francia and Cuadra 2010). The Mexican government intended to limit spending growth and reduce its public sector borrowing requirement to around 3 % of its GDP in 2011 and 2.5 % in 2012 (OECD 2011). Such active debt management had allowed for an improvement in its structure and helped Mexico to withstand the 2008 global financial crisis (Heritage 2012d). In addition, the federal government adopted measures aimed at ensuring efficient, timely and transparent public spending (ILO 2010c). Some public-sector prices at the federal and local levels were revised upward in 2010, particularly those for gasoline and gas that were frozen during 2009 to support the economy (Sanchez 2010). In addition, commercial operations are becoming more streamlined, and business formation is relatively efficient (Heritage 2012d).

Financial System

The Mexican banking system proved to be very resilient to the shocks facing the global financial system. Throughout the worst period of the financial crisis, Mexican banks continued to make profits with capitalization indices well above those required by law (Sidaoui, Ramos-Francia and Cuadra 2010). Mexico also implements a flexible financial system, such that when Mexican corporations find it difficult to obtain external financing, they are able to offset this restriction by issuing debt in the domestic markets (Sidaoui, Ramos-Francia and Cuadra 2010). In addition, the exchange-rate appreciation has helped to contain inflationary pressures (OECD 2011).

Fiscal Policy

In 2011, Mexico has already started to withdraw the fiscal stimulus of 2009 and increased taxes to calm market worries about fiscal trends (OECD 2011). During the financial crisis, Mexican fiscal consolidation package was implemented under an extremely adverse environment; however, it helped improve the country's fiscal position (Sidaoui, Ramos-Francia and Cuadra 2010). In addition, the Mexican Congress approved a fiscal reform that enables tax rates be adjusted to offset rising pension and social spending (Heritage 2012d; Sanchez 2010).

Employment

In 2011, Mexico enacted a new program to stimulate formal employment; the program offered an additional income tax deduction limited to 3 years for firms that create new jobs for workers who previously did not belong to the formal sector (OECD 2011).

Free Trade Agreements

Mexico has free trade agreements with over 50 countries, including Guatemala, Honduras, El Salvador, the European Free Trade Area, and Japan. It puts more than 90 % of its trade under free trade agreements (CIA 2012).

Technology Cluster

In Mexico, the technology cluster around the Tecnológico de Monterrey System has strengthened collaboration between academia and business. Monterrey's per capita GDP has grown 40 % faster than Mexico's in the past 10 years (Cadena et al. 2011). The city may become the growth engine of Mexico and set a model for future national development.

Venezuela

Even though there are comments about the Chavez Administration, Venezuela has the following characteristics that may support the country to future prospects.

1. The government benefitted from the rise in world oil prices, which sparked an economic boom and allowed Venezuelan government to increase expenditures on social programs with significantly reduced poverty levels (Sullivan 2011).
2. Venezuela occupies first place globally in certified oil reserves (Levy-Yeyati and Cohan 2011; Weisbrot 2010b).
3. Venezuela's large oil reserves enable the government to easily borrow internationally as necessary. For example, in 2010, China agreed to loan Venezuela US$20 billion in an advance payment for future oil deliveries (Weisbrot 2010a).

4. Due to its oil-generated surplus, Venezuela is well situated to resolve its macroeconomic problems and pursues a robust economic expansion (Weisbrot 2010a).
5. In the past decade, most of Venezuela's growth has been in the nonoil sector of the economy, and the private sector has grown faster than the public sector.
6. The poverty rate has been cut by more than half, from 54 % of households in the first half of 2003 to 26 % at the end of 2008. In addition, extreme poverty has fallen even more, by 72 %.
7. Inequality, as measured by the Gini index, has also fallen substantially. The index has fallen to 41 in 2008, from 48.1 in 2003 and 47 in 1999.
8. Real (inflation-adjusted) social spending per person more than tripled from 1998 to 2006.
9. There have been substantial gains in education, especially higher education, where gross enrollment rates more than doubled from 1999–2000 to 2007–2008.
10. The labor market also improved substantially over the last decade, with unemployment dropping from 11.3 to 7.8 % (Weisbrot, Ray and Sandoval 2009).

Challenges

In spite of suffering some loss of production capacity as a result of this global recession, Latin America has recovered its pre-crisis potential to grow. In 2012, the investment ratio in the region remained around 23.5 %, similar to the level before the 2009 contraction (Coutino, Fuentes and Leon 2012). However, these six countries still encounter some challenges that may hamper their future development. This section describes some, although not an exhaustive list, for readers' reference and exploration.

Argentina

Although Argentina had fast recovery from the 2008 global financial crisis, major challenges lying ahead including lasting high inflation, an overheating economy, high levels of unpredictable government intervention, institutional weaknesses, capital flight, massive government subsidies, and international macroeconomic framework.

Lasting High Inflation

The double-digit inflation in Argentina is becoming entrenched and raising doubts about the long-term viability of the government's growth-oriented economic policies. The biggest problem Argentina faces is that its inflation is higher than that of its trading partners, so the currency begins to appreciate in real terms (England 2011). Inflation also fuels wage demands, raising the risk of labor unrest as powerful trade unions negotiate salary hikes (Morales and Matthews 2011). In addition, the high inflation coupled with a moderate fall of the peso (Argentine currency) has resulted in the erosion of the competitiveness that the economy gained (England 2011). With the real value of the peso increased, imports become cheaper for Argentines and thus reduce the trade surplus (England 2011). With less money flowing into the country and access to foreign debt hindered since the 2001 default, there are growing concerns the government will not be able to maintain its spending without causing inflation to spiral upwards (England 2011).

Overheating Economy

The Argentine economy is overheating, based on the Economist's study (England 2011). The study rated all countries on a number of criteria—including inflation, unemployment, GDP growth, excess credit, real interest rates, and forecast change in current account balance. Argentina received a score of 100 %, putting the country top of the list, above other 'high-risk' nations such as Indonesia, Vietnam and Egypt (England 2011). Therefore, many economists predict 9 % growth is unsustainable in Argentina with high inflation and a deterioration of the trade balance (England 2011).

High Levels of Unpredictable Government Intervention

Argentina was criticized for its high levels of unpredictable government intervention—through subsidies, regulation, high inflation, and foreign trade tariffs (England 2011). For example, the government has increased regulatory intervention in recent years, undermining previous years' structural reforms that encouraged diversification and private investment. The government has continued to govern with a heavy hand with little tolerance for opponents, the state's role in the economy has also grown and the financial sector remains constrained by government influence (Heritage 2012a; The New York Times 2012). Such a trend reduces its attractiveness as a place to conduct business.

Institutional Weaknesses

Low quality of government institutions is a problem in Argentina (England 2011). Corruption and a weak judiciary continue to hold back Argentina's overall economic freedom and development (Heritage 2012a). After the financial crisis, the government has rapidly increased wages and subsidies, instead of improving Argentina's infrastructure, education, and health (England 2011). Erratic policies plus the high inflation rate make the country very risky for businesses to invest.

Capital Flight

Reportedly, US$73 billion, openly declared in the framework of the legal system, left Argentina for overseas during 2007–2011 (Melconian 2011). Data from United Nation also indicated that while US$26 billion has been invested in Argentina from abroad since 2007, over US$60 billion has been lost due to capital flight (England 2011). The gap shows that many Argentines do not trust in the local currency and demand US dollars. Through increased government controls and regulations in 2012, capital flight was temporarily reduced. However, the sense of uncertainty increased among consumers and businesses (Coutino, Fuentes and Leon 2012).

Government Massive Subsidies

The massive subsidies handed out by the government are the main problem faced by the Argentine economy and challenge its future evolution (Melconian 2011). Subsidies during the first half of 2011 totaled US$32.4 billion—a 73 % increase over the same period in 2010. Of this, around 59.5 % was spent on energy—specifically gas, diesel and electricity (England 2011). Such heavy government subsidizing of energy removes both the incentive for domestic investment in the sector and the reason for consumers to reduce consumption (England 2011). Many public services, such as transport and utilities, have been heavily subsidized for years and the cost of subsidizing energy has become an increasing burden due to soaring domestic demand.

International Macroeconomic Framework

Another challenge for the Argentine government is to accommodate economic policies to the new international macroeconomic and trade framework (ILO 2010a). In order to have better access to financial markets for the public and private sectors, the government needs to renew and restructure its remaining defaulted debt (ILO 2010a). Currently with no access to international markets, the government has resorted to the central bank for financing (Coutino, Fuentes and Leon 2012).

Brazil

For further national development, Brazil is keen to encourage foreign investment for long-term high growth. To build a strong, stable infrastructure, and good environment for foreign operations to take roots and for a better quality of life in Brazil, the following challenges are the areas that Brazilian government can pay more attention including, efficiency in government operations, rise in public spending, tax reform, social issues, and environmental issues.

Efficiency in Government Operations

According to OECD, Brazil is a big spender by emerging market standards and, in some respects, in comparison with OECD countries; however, the outcomes are not always commensurate with the level of spending (Gurria 2009). That means, there is ample space for enhancing efficiency in government operations. Therefore, investing in strengthening longer-term planning, effective implementation with appropriate evaluation criteria, and reducing rigidities in the budget should be emphasized. Progress in this area would allow policymakers to identify cost-effective programs, to secure adequate funding for these programs, and to strategically allocate budgetary resources.

Rise in Public Spending

In line with the effective utilization of national resources, another major challenge over the longer term for Brazil is the rise in public spending. General government spending (excluding interest payments) was nearly 32.5 % of its GDP in 2008 (Gurria 2009). Deducting the financial crisis stimulus package, this number still reflects above-average government spending. Experts warned the extraordinary rise in the cost of public employment, as the federal government needs to spend around 2 % of its GDP on it for a country with tax revenues of 36 % of the GDP (Mendonça 2010).

Tax Reform

Tax reform is also needed in Brazil to help open up the underground economy, encourage businesses to expand, and halt predatory industrial policies among the states (Gurria 2009). OECD proposes that the reform can include unifying the different value-added taxes administered by individual states, introducing a single system to replace the various federal levies on company turnover, and reducing taxes and social contributions on wages (Gurria 2009). Taxes and bureaucratic procedures that used to be taken for granted are now being examined with a more critical eye by the business sector that is keen to exploit efficiencies (Michener 2011). In addition, corruption and government waste that transfer to higher tax have also come under the close scrutiny. Thus, tax reform has become a big issue of public concern in Brazil when its economy relies more on exports and its industries need to have global competitiveness.

Social Issues

Socially, highly unequal income distribution and crime remain pressing problems in Brazil (CIA 2012). Poor quality of education, the worsening of the ports and transport infrastructure, high taxes and high electricity prices also weaken Brazil's competitiveness (Mendonça 2010). Another challenge is to incorporate a large segment of the population—the one-quarter of the population that lives on less than US$100 per month—into more productive and remunerative activities in the labor market (ILO 2010b).

Environmental Issues

Ecologically, environmental concerns will delay Brazil's progression to a developing country (CIA 2012). They include air and water pollution in Rio de Janeiro, Sao Paulo, and several other large cities; land degradation and water pollution caused by improper mining activities; wetland degradation; and severe oil spills. In addition, the deforestation in the Amazon Basin has destroyed the habitats and endangered a multitude of plant and animal species indigenous to the area. Furthermore, a lucrative illegal wildlife trade has deteriorated the forest ecology.

Chile

Although Chile weathered the 2008 global financial crisis very well and is the first country in South American to join OECD, it still faces some challenges including the need for a new national development paradigm, educational reform, job creation, reconstructing the nation, and poverty reduction.

The Need for a New National Development Paradigm

According to an interview with Chile's President Sebastian Pinera (Barton and Krell 2011), for a long time, there were three basic pillars for Chilean government: to have a stable, legitimate, democratic system; to have a free, open market economy, unencumbered by fiscal imbalances; and to have a state that works. Those pillars have successfully paved the way for what Chile is today, outperforming some of its Latin American neighbors. However, in the society of knowledge and information, President Pinera proposed that Chile should pursue four new pillars: to give a quality education to everyone, to invest in technology, to promote innovation and entrepreneurship, and to have a very flexible society and economy. He particularly highlighted that the world is changing, and Chile has to be ready to adapt, to take advantage of the opportunities, and to adjust to the changes that come from abroad.

Educational Reform

In 2006, the Chilean government experienced a massive student strike (named the "penguin revolt"), called to protest the quality of the Chilean educational system (Briones 2010). Under the government's pledge, Chile is going to undertake a huge educational reform—trying to fix a system that hasn't worked because it was caught up by all kinds of interest groups in the past (Barton and Krell 2011).

Job Creation

Chile has a very high unemployment rate. The country has mapped a plan to triple its investment in technology as a percentage of its GDP, promoting innovation and entrepreneurship, including within the public sector, and trying to build a more flexible and adaptive economy and society for job creation over time. In addition, it plans for a huge influx of women into the labor force. As a result, it is essential for Chile to create jobs for them—an estimated one million over the next 4 years—to achieve the level of female labor force participation in other OECD countries (Barton and Krell 2011).

Reconstructing the Nation

It is challenging for Chile to reconstruct the nation, due to the huge costs of rebuilding what was destroyed by the February 2010 earthquake and the tsunami that came after. Chile lost one-third of its schools and hospitals and suffered enormous damage to bridges, airports, and ports—all adding up to US$30 billion in losses, which is roughly 18 % of its GDP (Barton and Krell 2011).

Poverty Reduction

According to diagnosis, the most important causes of poverty in Chile are the lack of equality in education, weakness in creating good jobs, and weaknesses in the family (Barton and Krell 2011). These concerns pose long-term challenges for effective poverty reduction.

Colombia

Colombia faces the following challenges in the years to come: poverty and inequality, fiscal policy, public policies, infrastructure, and environmental issues.

Poverty and Inequalities

In Colombia, extreme poverty and inequalities have not been eradicated by the country's robust economic growth and continue to demand targeted measures from the State and the investor community (SECO 2009).

Fiscal Policy

Due to a weak fiscal structure, Colombia needs to enforce rules to encourage fiscal savings and make sure spending evolves with long-term fiscal revenues. The country has to adopt structural tax reforms to reduce tax exemptions, increase taxable bases, and improve tax administration. It can also develop fiscal policy by improving consistency in spending and revenue policies with macroeconomic stability. In addition, the government can encourage social support programs and stabilize mining and energy income (Economy Watch 2010).

Public Policies

Public policy in Colombia has not been growth-oriented in key areas such as infrastructure and transportation. As a result, public investments have been decreasing for a long time (Economy Watch 2010). Further growth in economic freedom in Colombia will require deeper institutional reforms that include better protection of property rights and a stronger judicial system. Corruption remains considerable in many sectors of the economy, and the relatively high marginal tax rates encourage tax evasion (Heritage 2012c). In addition, the infiltration of the business community by money laundering (from kidnappings and cocaine trafficking) and pyramid investment schemes is a phenomenon that needs to be dealt with (SECO 2009).

Infrastructure

Colombia faces specific challenges in infrastructure. With its high rate of urbanization, most of the economic potential as well as its social and ecological problems are concentrated in the big cities. The bottlenecks in transport could pose avoidable limitations to domestic growth, corporate profits of emerging MNEs, job creation, and GDP growth (Garces 2011). Innovative solutions are needed to address the issues of transportation, waste, water and energy to revive the spluttering economy. The need to catch up in urban infrastructure, combined with limited revenue-raising potential, will challenge cities' financial management in the years to come (SECO 2009).

Environmental Issues

To a certain extent, Colombia's rapid economic growth of recent years has been to the detriment of the environment. Therefore, Colombia faces the challenge of encouraging sustainable investment by taking into account ecological externalities in economic decision-making (SECO 2009). Policy reforms are needed that can optimize investments in oil and gas, at the same time encourage corporate social responsibility with a positive environmental impact (Garces 2011). In particular, Colombia must continue to strengthen its environmental impact assessment (EIA) system, also to ensure a more effective application of EIA international standards in the public and private sectors, including FDI outflows by Colombian MNEs (Garces 2011). Although Colombia has promulgated laws regulating the environmental impact of commercial activity, it still needs to widen the scope of legal measures. Administrative support and procedures for the design and implementation of environmental impact systems with control mechanisms are also needed.

Mexico

As the Mexican economy recovers, ongoing economic and social concerns include outdated infrastructure and labor laws, low real wages, underemployment for a large segment of the population, inequitable income distribution, few advancement opportunities, and weak private investment in the energy sector (CIA 2012). Challenges described hereunder report the most commonly mentioned concerns, including fiscal system, financial system, heavy reliance on the U.S. economy, structural reforms, energy subsidies, education system, informal sector, monopoly, oil technology, and social policies.

Fiscal System

Another problem is lax local administrations and enforcement of taxes, mainly because of weak incentives to collect higher taxes. Therefore, the Mexican government can consider strengthening tax enforcement through extended use of risk models, considering a requalification after some years or a sunset clause, training tax collectors or offering attractive pay with career paths (OECD 2011). Another agenda would be withdrawing zero rates and exemptions within the VAT system, entrusting subnational governments to increase their own tax revenues, and evaluating the in-work tax credit (OECD 2011).

Financial System

For Mexico, building-up foreign exchange assets through a rules-based mechanism and moving toward macro-prudential financial regulation and supervision are suggested (OECD 2011). The budget surpluses accruing during economic upswings or periods of high oil prices should be accumulated in a stabilization fund (OECD 2011). As the first step, simple and transparent rules on savings and withdrawals would enhance the transparency of oil revenue management. Further reforms of financial supervision would also contribute to macroeconomic stability. Vigilance is needed as some inflationary risks have re-emerged as the economic recovery gains strength faster than expected (OECD 2011).

Heavy Reliance on the U.S. Economy

Promoting export diversification, such as through multilateral and regional trade agreements is important for Mexico. In 2009, the United States accounts for half of Mexico's imports, 80 % of its exports, and most of its foreign investment and remittances income (Nanto 2009). Greater geographical and product diversification of exports would reduce Mexico's exposure to sudden changes in U.S. economic conditions (OECD 2011). Mexico's dependence on the U.S. economy diminishes its ability to diversify its markets and limits the extent of Mexico's long-term potential for economic growth (Villarreal 2010).

Structural Reforms

Mexico's weak potential growth performance and slow convergence toward average OECD living standards highlight the need for structural reforms (OECD 2011; Sanchez 2010). Structural reforms should address the issues of macroeconomic volatility, limited competition in a number of sectors, and weaknesses within the education system. In the longer term, further tax and oil sector reform will be needed to make the budget less dependent on oil revenues and their volatility (OECD 2011). As a result, a wide range of transformations is desirable, including a fiscal reform that efficiently broadens the tax base, public security, protection of property rights and physical infrastructure, and the liberalization of barriers to entrepreneurial activities (Sanchez 2010). Some of the structural reforms proposed by the government in September 2009 have deep-seated political implications. However, they were strongly opposed by the major political parties, such as restructuring the energy sector and the labor and fiscal reforms (Villarreal 2010).

Energy Subsidies

Mexican energy subsidies are inefficient as a poverty-alleviation mechanism, as a large part is captured by higher-income groups. Moreover, energy subsidies create incentives to consume more energy and invest less in energy efficiency, reducing energy security, and raising greenhouse gas (GHG) emissions (OECD 2011).

Education System

One key weakness of the Mexican education system is the qualification of teachers and principals. Therefore, a nationwide evaluation system for teacher performance and accreditation standards for teacher-training institutions is needed (OECD 2011). In addition, resources reallocation to provide schools with reliable financing and professionalize the selection of principals to assume greater responsibility for teacher employment and school management is also important (OECD 2011).

Informal Sector

Mexico's informal sector, which is large by OECD standards, is a drag on productivity growth (OECD 2011). Better education, enhanced regulation, and improved incentives to formalize are key reforms to combat informality. A stronger enforcement of labor and tax laws will assist the formalization as well. In addition, the government should continue its efforts to reduce costs of starting and running a business, the costs of employing workers formally, and to reduce regulatory hurdles that hinder formalization (OECD 2011). It should also strengthen the value of the mandatory social security package for low-wage workers (OECD 2011).

Monopoly with Limited Competition

One of Mexico's primary challenges in making its economy more efficient and increasing productivity is the issue of monopolies and limited competition

(Villarreal 2010). The influence and power of the federal government, the energy-intensive industrial firms, and the industry's labor union have prevented change from taking place in the oil sector. Telecommunications sector is another area that is frequently mentioned as not having enough competition and being controlled by a monopoly (Villarreal 2010). Some also argue that another challenge to the Mexican economy is the powerful labor unions, which has a monopoly on hiring, firing, and collective bargaining and exert a great deal of influence in the energy and healthcare industries and, most importantly, in education (Villarreal 2010). To cope with the issue, the OECD has cooperated with Mexican Ministry of Economy to develop a reform agenda. The recently adopted competition law reform is an important step toward reducing market power of incumbents across all industries.

Oil Technology

Oil production in Mexico has been reduced. Even though the production has stabilized after the financial crisis, maintaining current production levels beyond 10 years would require continued substantial investments in high-cost exploration and new discoveries (OECD 2011). Mexico can collaborate with other countries and take advantage of worldwide technological progress (Sanchez 2010).

Social Policies

Mexico needs to maintain growth-enhancing investments and social policies to catch up with average OECD living standards through reducing poverty and creating jobs (CIA 2012; OECD 2011). In addition, there are longer-term fiscal sustainability challenges related to population aging and the associated increase in costs for the states' defined pension and healthcare systems (OECD 2011). To have a sustainable healthcare system, the Mexican government should consider reform the different healthcare systems, moving toward integrated financing of a basic universal healthcare insurance, either through taxes or fees (OECD 2011).

Other social policies of concern include easing procedures to dismiss workers based on poor performance or redundancy (OECD 2011), corruption, labor market rigidity, the judicial system which is slow to resolve cases and vulnerable to corruption (Heritage 2012d). Another serious challenge is the organized crime and drug trafficking. The escalation of related violence has resulted in increased risk aversion and reduced foreign investment flows (Villarreal 2010). Reportedly, it has trimmed an estimated 1.2 percentage points from Mexico's GDP (Heritage 2012d).

Venezuela

The main challenge for Venezuela in the next couple of years is to keep the economy on a steady growth path. Investing in infrastructure and public projects will also help increase productivity (Weisbrot, Ray and Sandoval 2009). There are a number of challenges that may impede Venezuela's future national development including heavy dependency on oil products, financial system, economic downturn, nationalization, low foreign investment, and social issues.

Heavy Dependency on Oil Products

Venezuela's heavy dependency on oil products has weakened the domestic productive system for tradable goods, particularly in the industrial and agricultural industrial sectors (Levy-Yeyati and Cohan 2011).

Financial System

Monetary stability is weak as the financial situation of the Venezuelan economy can be affected by a sudden withdrawal of private financial flows, by a major increase in the cost of foreign loans, or by a decrease in the net foreign investment in fixed assets. However, there is no sign of a firm decision to adopt countercyclical policies, due to a lack of "fiscal space"—funds or resources to stabilize the cycle (Vera Azaf 2010). The government's biggest long-term economic mistake has been the maintenance of a fixed, overvalued exchange rate (Weisbrot 2010a, b). Although the government devalued the currency in January 2010, from 2.15 to 4.3 to the dollar for most official foreign exchange transactions, the currency is still overvalued (Weisbrot 2010b). An overvalued currency—by making imports artificially cheap and the country's exports more expensive—hurts Venezuela's nonoil tradable goods' sectors and prevents the economy from diversifying away from oil (Weisbrot 2010b).

Economic Downturn

Despite the availability of the rich natural resource and record-breaking oil prices within the last decade, Venezuela is experiencing one of the worst economic downturns in its recent history. The country's economy has contracted in significant ways over the last 5 years (Rodriguez 2011). If oil stays at US$100 a barrel, Venezuela's export revenues should just cover its foreign-exchange requirements—US$11 billion of debt service, US$28 billion of capital flight, and US$100 billion of imports—over 2012–2013 (The Economist 2011). In addition, blackouts and power outages have become a norm (Anees 2010).

Nationalization

Venezuela has nationalized hundreds of companies and trumped up charges against their owners, causing much of Venezuela's private sector to close up shop and flee. Some companies have been nationalized without compensation and without appropriate legal procedures being followed (Sullivan 2011). By estimation, Venezuelan bourgeoisie has closed 4,000 large- or medium-sized enterprises during the last 10 years (Larsen 2009). As a result, the country has seen vast capital flight, and must import many goods that it used to produce (The Economist 2011). Economic freedom in Venezuela has been severely hampered by state interference, and the economy is increasingly stagnant and there are price controls on almost all goods and services (Heritage 2012e).

Low Foreign Investment

Venezuela's low levels of FDI are an expression of its incoherent macroeconomic management, the negative business environment resulting from its current model of development and its economic dependence on oil rents (Levy-Yeyati and Cohan 2011).

Social Issues

Public employees have staged frequent protests over unpaid salaries, worsening conditions, and a virtual freeze on collective bargaining (The Economist 2011). The public sector is bloated and inefficient, and the informal economy is growing. Corruption is rampant under an inefficient judicial system that is vulnerable to political influence. Contracts and property rights are not well respected, and government expropriations have been on the rise. In 2009, education "reform" targeted religious educators and parochial school funding and reduced the autonomy of university administrators (Heritage 2012e).

Policy Implications

The main cause of economic downturn in these six Latin American countries during the past few years was not the financial crisis; it was the spillover effect of the drastic decrease of export demands and the drop of oil and commodity prices that these countries mainly rely on. None of the banking sector of these countries faltered during the crisis, as generally they carry conservative financial regulations, follow international capitalization standards, and maintain relatively low levels of debt. The resilience of their current financial system is the results of continuous structural reforms after several painful financial crises during the past few decades.

As a result, when the international trade gradually recovered from early 2010 and the oil and commodity prices revived, their economies rebounded quickly.

The intangible national intellectual capital (NIC)—human capital, market capital, process capital, and renewal capital are the so-called "soft power" of a nation. In any nation, people, systems, and governance—the main ingredients of NIC are always key success factors of a government. Rich and poor countries alike possess NIC, only to different degrees. Based on the data of 48 countries, the result that the higher the NIC the higher the GDP per capita (ppp) presented in Fig. 3.7 indicates the value of NIC. Although the NIC of these six countries is comparatively low among the 48 countries, important implications are disclosed through the tables and figures reported in this booklet. They provide valuable information for the policy makers to look back on the national intangibles before the global financial crisis, observe their co-development with the GDP during and after the crisis, and then draw lessons from it.

By investigating economic development and NIC development from 2005 to 2010, we have been able to connect the co-evolution of tangibles and intangibles for the six Latin American countries. Implications that can be drawn from our research findings are as follows:

First, national intellectual capital development goes together with the economic development and should be regarded as an enhancer of economic growth. The co-development of NIC and GDP presented in Fig. 3.7 indicates that the higher the NIC the higher the GDP per capita (ppp), meaning NIC development generally accompanies with GDP growth. The much praised Brazilian development with its resilience during this global financial crisis is evidenced in its gaining relatively large-scale market capital and renewal capital international competitiveness exhibited in Figs. 3.19 and 3.20. On the contrary, Mexico's deepest GDP slide, increasing government debt and unemployment (Figs. 2.1–2.3) agree with its losing NIC international competiveness displayed in Figs. 3.25 and 3.26. Therefore, attending to the development of NIC should help policy makers gain different perspectives on national development and identify some early signs for timely coping strategies.

Second, Latin American countries can utilize their relatively good short-term NIC—market capital and process capital to boost national development. From the co-development of various capitals with GDP (Figs. 3.8–3.12), most of the development paths of these countries (except market capital and process capital of Chile) are at the bottom corner of the graphs. That is, their NIC and GDP are both low among the 48 countries. However, a promising sign is their short-term NIC—market capital and process capital—presented in Figs. 3.15 and 3.16. The co-development paths of these two short-term NIC for the six countries spread from low (Argentina and Venezuela), to middle (Brazil, Colombia, and Mexico), and high (Chile) on the graphs. In addition, the development forms a potential value chain of low, middle, and high levels. Therefore, countries in this group can capitalize such relative competitiveness by increasing trade within the region to reinforce each other's market capital and co-construct important infrastructure or co-establish better governance system for boosting each other's process capital with the convenience of geographical proximity.

Third, national intellectual capital keeps nonoil export countries competitive, as in the case of Chile. Latin America is an oil rich region. For the countries reported in this booklet, the world ranking of oil exports is Argentina 27, Brazil 13, Colombia 26, Mexico 7, and Venezuela 12, respectively (CIA 2012). Chile is the only country that does not have oil exports and oil reserves, although it is the world's number one copper export country. The oil-export countries benefited from high oil prices (except a short period during the financial crisis) and used the surplus to weather this global financial storm with relative ease, even though their NIC was low. However without oil, Chile has created its own competitiveness through developing its market capital (ranks 5 out of 48), process capital (ranks 28 out of 48), aggressive international trade, strong fiscal policy, and proper management of sovereign wealth funds accumulated during periods of high copper prices and economic growth. As a result, Chile is the first South American country to join OECD. It also has the highest NIC scores and the best 6-year average GDP per capita (ppp) in this country cluster, beating out the oil-rich countries. The intangibles mentioned above evidently play a certain role in creating Chile's competiveness.

Fourth, positive national intellectual capital ranking changes reflect national competiveness. Chapter 3 reports each country's NIC internal and external comparisons. Internal comparison shows a country's yearly score changes over 6 years 2005–2010 (Figs. 3.1–3.5); whereas external comparison reports ranking changes on 48 countries over three time periods (Table 3.2 and Figs. 3.17–3.28). Colombia is the best example to show the implication of ranking changes. From Table 3.1, Colombia holds the second highest NIC score among these six countries, its individual capital scores (Figs. 3.1–3.5) did not change too much over the 6 years. However, Table 3.2 showed quite a number of ranking declines (negative numbers), representing loss of international competitiveness in those areas. Such a phenomenon agrees with Colombia's Global Competiveness Index (Fig. 1.1), which dropped 13 ranks from 55 to 68. In addition, its 6-year GDP per capita (ppp) average is the lowest among the six countries. In other words, Colombia does not follow the norm of the higher the NIC, the higher the GDP per capita (ppp) presented in Fig. 3.7 . Its NIC ranking declines over three time periods explains its vulnerability. Therefore, countries cannot be too complacent on self-improvement; true competitiveness is tested in an international arena. The dynamic change of international competitiveness, even for intangible NIC can be monitored for timely coping strategies.

Fifth, government related issues constitute a major part of impeding factors in achieving GDP growth. Table 3.3 summarizes the main enhancing and impeding factors of GDP growth for each country. Among the impeding factors, government related issues have the largest total counts (19), followed by market capital and R&D issues (12 each), and human capital issues (10). Government related indicators include capital availability, transparency of government policy, convenience of establishing new firms, fair business competition environment, and government efficiency. Capital availability problem of Argentina, Colombia, and Venezuela has been transferred from impeding factor to enhancing factor after the financial crisis with the oil price increase and the stimulus plans. Other government-related issues provide a good guideline for each individual country to strategize future national development policies.

Sixth, research and development investment should lead to further national development in this region. Table 3.4 summarizes the first five efficiency drivers of each country, benchmarking Germany. The efficiency drivers of these six countries are quite similar. Among the eight common drivers, five of them are R&D related. In other words, to achieve the level of Germany, these countries need to focus more on basic research, IP rights protection, patents per capita, R&D % GDP, and university-enterprise cooperation. This message is particularly important for Chile, as Chile has achieved a good level of market capital and process capital; however, its renewal capital and GDP per capita (ppp) are still relatively low. For the next stage development, Chile needs to enhance the added value of its intangible and tangible assets. R&D is one effective way to achieve the goal.

Seventh, oil- and commodity-dependent countries need national intellectual capital to facilitate national development and establish better governance systems for a more resilient economy free from the risk of external shock. Common sense leads to the assumption that oil rich countries should be wealthy enough to improve the common good, such as social welfare, good education, and poverty reduction. However, the situation of the two oil-rich countries in this group—Mexico and Venezuela does not fit such an assumption. They still have a large population below the poverty line and suffer from low quality education. Their 6-year average GDP per capita (ppp) is very low, compared with other oil rich countries like Saudi Arabia or Qatar. For another comparison, Chile had the foresight to prudently manage its sovereign wealth fund from copper and aggressively develop free trade agreements to lessen the global financial impact and increase its national wellbeing. A preliminary observation is that the tangible commodity is not the key; the most important factor is how the precious natural resources are developed and managed to maximize their values for national wellbeing. In other words, the development and management—the intangibles are even more important than the product itself. NIC ranking changes of Mexico and Venezuela presented in Figs. 3.25–3.28 indicate ranking declines in most time periods, reflecting their weak NIC and loss of NIC international competitiveness after the financial crisis. The NIC results reported in this volume show a clear direction that policy makers of oil and commodity dependent countries can work on.

Eighth, Argentina's good performance during the global financial crisis may pave the way for its future development. Several indicators show that Argentina was performing relatively well during this global financial crisis. Its real GDP growth was still positive in 2009 and had the largest rebound (8.13 %) in 2010 among the six countries (Fig. 2.1), general government debt reduced from 85.42 % in 2005 to 47.09 % in 2010 (Fig. 2.2), and the unemployment rate reduced from 11.5 to 7.3 % for the same period (Fig. 2.3). It is also the only country that has all positive NIC ranking changes, comparing the most recent period (2009–2010) with the 6-year average ranking; that is, Argentina gained NIC international competitiveness after the financial crisis. The problem is its consumer price index increase, from 9.64 % in 2005 to 10.57 % in 2010 (Fig. 5). However, its overall NIC ranking covering 2005–2010 is second to last among the six countries (45 out of 48, Table 3.1), surpassed only Venezuela. Its Global Competitiveness Index declines 13 ranks from 72 to 85 (Fig. 1.1). With Argentina's better standing after the 2008 financial crisis, working on NIC development for building a more resilient and advanced economy should be a worthwhile investment.

Concluding Remarks and Emerging Insights

During the 2008 global financial crisis, the global economy underwent an economic contraction unseen in the recent past. In the aftermath, speed of recovery varies in different parts of the world. Stepping into 2013, the global economic outlook is promising. Global growth is projected to increase during 2013 (European Commission 2012; IMF 2013). Major policy decisions have laid the foundations for a strengthening in confidence and acute crisis risk has been reduced in the Euro area and the United States.

However in the Euro zone, the return to recovery after a protracted contraction is delayed and the downside risks remain significant, including renewed setbacks in the Euro area (IMF 2013). In 2012, the U.S. economy was growing but performance remained below what was expected. In China, India and Brazil, production growth was also slowing down due to both a reduction in export and lower domestic spending (CPB 2012; Elliott 2012). Recovery from the Latin American region is pretty well. The region is in position to perform according to its potential capacity, growing around 4 % was predicted in 2013, assuming the global economy does not deteriorate further (Coutino, Fuentes and Leon 2012).

In general, financial crises have been generated by factors such as an overshooting of markets, excessive leveraging of debt, credit booms, miscalculations of risk, rapid outflows of capital from a country, mismatches between asset types (e.g., short-term dollar debt used to fund long-term local currency loans), unsustainable macroeconomic policies, off-balance sheet operations by banks, inexperience with new financial instruments, and deregulation without sufficient market monitoring and oversight (Nanto 2009).

In the wake of the crisis, a new surveillance mechanism is in place to initiate necessary procedure and propose economic sanctions on noncompliance. Important legislative changes are also underway in many countries to improve the surveillance of imbalances and to help ensure that the necessary corrective action is undertaken where risks emerge (Barnes 2010). Alongside with planned structural reforms, macroeconomic, financial, and fiscal management would be strengthened in an integrated way (Barnes 2010) in order to reap the best result. Some countries have also been experimenting with creating an independent fiscal council to monitor and assess official fiscal projections. Furthermore, structural reform efforts were made to use more output-based performance measures and to choose the measures with care to avoid distorting incentives. In general, efforts of strengthening national governance is undergoing in many parts of the world after this global financial crisis.

Financial crises of some kind occur sporadically every decade in various locations around the world. Each financial crisis is unique, yet each bears some resemblance to others as well (Nanto 2009). The main lesson drawn from this financial crisis is that there are no substitutes for good and well-coordinated economic policies. Prudent macroeconomic measures together with a well-capitalized financial system and flexible exchange rates are suitable elements to preserve the confidence of market participants and facilitate an orderly adjustment to external disturbances (Sanchez 2010).

As a recap, to counter worsening economic conditions worldwide, a total of US$2 trillion in stimulus packages, amounting to approximately 3 % of the world gross domestic product, has been allocated (some of the packages include measures that extend into subsequent years), an amount that exceeds the call by the International Monetary Fund (IMF) for fiscal stimulus totaling 2 % of the global GDP. IMF also estimated that as of January 2009, the U.S. fiscal stimulus packages as a percentage of the GDP in 2009 would amount to 1.9 %, for the euro area 0.9 %, for Japan 1.4 %, for Asia excluding Japan 1.5 % and for the rest of the G-20 countries 1.1 % (Nanto 2009).

Latin American region becomes more integrated to the world economy. As emerging markets have grown, Western financial institutions have increased their investments in emerging markets. According to report, G-10 financial institutions have a total of $4.7 trillion of exposure to emerging markets with $1.6 trillion to Central and Eastern Europe, $1.5 trillion to emerging Asia, and $1.0 trillion to Latin America (Nanto 2009). These six Latin American countries were resilient to the 2008 global financial crisis. However to prepare for future, questions such as "How exposed will Latin America to future global recession?" and "How can the region best prepare itself for such an unfavorable environment?" need to be asked (Levy-Yeyati and Cohan 2011).

In terms of future NIC development, our other study on the top 10 NIC ranking countries reveals that the interplay among the four capitals—human capital, market capital, process capital, and renewal capital—resulted in the best synergetic prospect for GDP growth. When their weaker capital (process capital) interacts with stronger capital (market capital), both effects on the GDP are enhanced (Lin 2011). This finding prompts our suggestion for the Latin American countries to enhance their economies by capitalizing on their relatively competitive short-term NIC—market capital and process capital.

Overall, NIC intelligence suggests that in an era when the intangible asset has become a key competitive advantage, investing in NIC development is basically investing in future national development. Transparent information from multiple perspectives, including the NIC intelligence reported in this volume, will enable decision makers to have better sensibility in preventing a similar situation from happening again.

Appendix 1
Summary of the Main Stimulus Packages of the Six Latin American Countries

C. Y.-Y. Lin et al., *National Intellectual Capital and the Financial Crisis in Argentina, Brazil, Chile, Colombia, Mexico, and Venezuela*, SpringerBriefs in Economics,
DOI: 10.1007/978-1-4614-8921-4,

Country	Date	Amount	Item
Argentina	Nov. 26, 2008 (around 3.9 %)	#1 US$32bn (ARS111bn)	To boost spending on public works to US$32bn (ARS111bn), up from the US$21.2bn (ARS71bn). About US$17bn (ARS57bn) of the stimulus package (up 50 % from last year) was budgeted for 2009, ranging from schools to highways projects
	Dec. 4, 2008	#2 #3 US$3.9bn (ARS13.2bn)	US$3.9bn (ARS13.2bn) to spur the country's consumption and exports
			Reduced-interest loans for consumers, companies and export financing. 5 % cut in export taxes on wheat and corn
	Dec. 11, 2008	#1 US$88mn (ARS300mn)	US$88mn (ARS300mn) to stimulate domestic tourism
Brazil	Sept. 2008	#5	1. Public bank could purchase the stock of real estate firms and other sectors (US$880mn—US$1.09bn)
			2. Loans to companies for refinancing their external debts (US$20bn)
	(around 0.2 %)		3. On January 21, 2009, the central bank cut its basic rate by 100 basis points (from 13.75 to 12.75 %)
			4. Expansion of borrowing capacity of PETROBRAS (a semi-public Brazilian multinational energy corporation) and the National bank (BNDES) to keep up planned investment levels (US$5.3bn)
			5. US$6.5bn in support for the agricultural sector
			6. A 12 % increase in the minimum wage and 14 % increase in the health and education sectors
	Dec. 23, 2008	#6 US$5bn	Tax cuts for capital goods producers and personal computers
		#5	Fiscal Policy
		See the right column	1. Injection of over US$43.8bn to keep up consumption levels
			2. Ensure a budget of at least US$11.4bn for spending
			3. The sectors worst hit by the crisis were granted fresh tax cuts and more resources
			4. US$9.2bn earmarked for the Growth Acceleration Program in the 2009 budget
			5. US$6.3bn reserved for the Sovereign Fund on projects
			6. Release US$17.5bn to help Brazilian firms get raw materials
			7. A series of tax cuts totaling around US$3.7bn to boost consumption
			8. Extra US$4.2bn of government investment, in addition to the US$16.6bn already planned
			9. US$2.5bn Treasury Bond for infrastructure investments

(continued)

(continued)

Country	Date	Amount	Item
		#7 US$221.4bn	Earmarked for infrastructure building focusing on transport system and energy segment
	2009	#8 US$20bn (1.2 % GDP) in 2009	1. Infrastructure investment (41.5 %), including My house, My Life housing program for low- and middle-income households
			2. Tax cuts (35 %)
			3. Interest rate subsidies (15.5 %)
			4. Extraordinary budget transfers to municipalities (5.5 %)
			5. Extension of the Family Fund (1.5 %)
			6. Extension of unemployment insurance benefits (1 %)
	Mar. 2009	#8 #9 US$19bn (BRL34bn)—1.2 % of GDP US$40bn (BRL72bn)	Budget for new homes for low-and middle-income families was increased from US$19bn to US$40bn (BRL72bn)
		#4	The Brazilian Treasury reacted by speeding up revenue expenditure through increasing the public sector payroll and increasing social security spending and transfers to the private sector
	2009	#10	Reduced deposit requirements, bought portfolios from smaller banks, and provide loans to micro- and small enterprises
			Public banks provided about 41 % of all loans (18.5 % of GDP). Reduced the basic interest rate to its lowest level in over 20 years (8.75 %, equivalent to a real annual rate of less than 5 %)
			As of Sep. 2009, total loans represented 45.7 % of GDP
	March—4th quarter, 2009	#10	Temporarily reduced the industrial products tax on automobile sales, household electrical appliances and construction inputs. Lower income tax rates were introduced for middle-income families
			Extended payment deadlines for various taxes
		#10 US$9bn (BRL20.5bn)	Federal government investment rose 12.7 %, reaching US$9bn (BRL20.5bn)

(continued)

(continued)

Country	Date	Amount	Item
Chile	Nov. 2008	#12 US$1.15bn	US$1.15bn package—loans to middle-income families and small and medium-sized businesses
	Jan. 5 2009 (around 2.3 %)	#11 #13 #14 US$4bn (as 2.8 % of 2008 GDP)	US$4bn for infrastructure, subsidies, and tax rebates, including
			• US$1.5bn towards tax rebates and subsidies
			• $1.5bn towards higher public spending
			• $1bn to a state-owned copper company, Codelco, to finance investments
			• tax cuts for small business owners
			• increase 100,000 jobs
	Feb. 12, 2009	#15	Reduced its benchmark interest rate by a massive 2.5–4.75 %
	May-09	#11	
		1. US$700mn, 0.5 % of 2008 GDP	1. For infrastructure
		2. US$8.8mn, 0.01 % of 2008 GDP	2. For science, R&D and innovation
		3. $147mn, 0.1 % of 2008 GDP	3. For education
Colombia	11-May-09	#16 US$10.5bn	The IMF approved a one-year, US$10.5bn credit line for Colombia
	Aug. 2009	#17 US$1bn	The U.S.-Colombian Trade Promotion Agreement (TPA) provided "free" economic stimulus through increasing U.S. exports of around US$1bn without adding to the federal budget deficit
	9-May-11	#18 US$6.2bn	The IMF approved a new US$6.2bn credit line for Colombia
Mexico	Mar. 2008 (around 4.7 %)	#19 US$5.6bn	Utility rates discounts, tax breaks, infrastructure development, housing, agriculture and diversification of exports
	Jan. 2009	#20 #21 US$54bn	US$54bn economic recovery plan, including freezing gasoline prices, boosting spending on public works, and allocating US$42bn for infrastructure
Venezuela	Aug. 10, 2011	#22	Venezuela mainly elevated its international reserves worth close to US$30bn and diversified its oil export markets to reduce financial impact (Venezuela had large surplus and did not require stimulus during this financial crisis)

number of reference

1. MercoPress (2008) Argentina bolsters size of the stimulus package to 32 b. USD, Dec 16. http://en.mercopress.com/2008/12/16/argentina-bolsters-size-of-the-stimulus-package-to-32-b-usd
2. Faries B (2008) Fernandez unveils stimulus plan for Argentine economy, Bloomberg, Dec 4. http://www.bloomberg.com/apps/news?pid=newsarchive&sid=aNtgy0br55Ag
3. Khatiwada S (2009) Stimulus package to counter global economic crisis: a review. International Institute for Labour Studies, Discussion paper DP/196/2009. http://www.ilo.org/public/english/bureau/inst/publications/discussion/dp19609.pdf
4. Mendonça de Barros JR (2010) The impact of the international financial crisis on Brazil (ARI). Real Instituto Elcano. http://www.realinstitutoelcano.org/wps/portal/

rielcano_eng/Content?WCM_GLOBAL_CONTEXT=/elcano/elcano_in/zonas_in/cooperation+developpment/ari38-2010

5. Valadão M, Porto NG (2009) Brazilian Response to International Financial Crisis, the Pre-Salt Discoveries by Petrobras and the New Free Trade Areas in the Cities of Brazil. Law Bus Rev Am 15:673–674

6. Nanto DK (2009) Global financial crisis: analysis and policy implications, Congressional Research Service, Oct 2. http://www.fas.org/sgp/crs/misc/RL34742.pdf

7. Economy Watch (2010a) Brazil economic stimulus package, June 30. http://www.economywatch.com/economic-stimulus-package/brazil.html

8. International Labour Office (ILO) (2010) G20 country briefs: Brazil's response to the crisis. G20 Meeting of Labour and Employment Ministers, Washington, D.C. 20–21 April 2010. http://www.dol.gov/ilab/media/events/G20_ministersmeeting/G20-brazil-brief.pdf

9. Novacich SE (2011) Minha casa minha vida development. The Rio Times, May 17. http://riotimesonline.com/brazil-news/front-page/minha-casa-minha-vida-development/#

10. Economic Commission for Latin America and the Caribbean (ECLAC) (2009) Preliminary overview of the economies of Latin America and the Caribbean 2009, pp 78–80. http://www.eclac.org/publicaciones/xml/3/38063/Brazil.pdf

11. OECD (2009) Policy responses to the economic crisis: investing in innovation for long-term growth, June 2009. http://www.oecd.org/dataoecd/59/45/42983414.pdf12. Luksic D (2009) Chile update: effects of the global economic crisis. Americas Society, Feb 12. http://www.as-coa.org/article.php?id=1481

13. The New York Times (2009) Chile announces $4 billion stimulus for jobs and copper miner, Jan 6. http://www.nytimes.com/2009/01/06/business/worldbusiness/06iht-chile.1.19110322.html

14. International Business Wiki (n.d.) Chile's economy and stimulus package, Wikia. http://internationalbusiness.wikia.com/wiki/Chile's_Economy_and_Stimulus_Package

15. The Economist (2009) Stimulating: cashing in the fruits of rigour, Feb 19. http://www.economist.com/node/13145570?story_id=13145570

16. Monsters and Critics (2009) IMF approves 10.5-billion-dollar credit line for Colombia, May 11. http://news.monstersandcritics.com/americas/news/article_1476497.php/IMF_approves_10_5-billion-dollar_credit_line_for_Colombia

17. Wolf B (2009) Colombia trade pact: free stimulus. Latin Business Chronicle, Aug 20. https://www.latinbusinesschronicle.com/app/article.aspx?id=3617

18. International Monetary Fund (IMF) (2011) IMF Approves $6.2 billion credit line for Colombia, May 9. http://www.imf.org/external/pubs/ft/survey/so/2011/car050911a.htm

19. Economy Watch (2010b) Mexico economic stimulus package, June 30. http://www.economywatch.com/economic-stimulus-package/mexico.html

20. Cevallos D (2009) Stimulus plan to curb impact of crisis. Inter Press Service News Agency, Jan 7. http://ipsnews.net/news.asp?idnews=45329

21. Wilson Center Expert Sources (2009) Mexico's stimulus plan comes at a critical time. Mexico Institute of the Woodrow Wilson International Center for Scholars, Aug 1. http://mexicoinstitute.wordpress.com/2009/01/08/mexicos-stimulus-plan-comes-at-a-critical-time/

22. Reardon J (2011) Venezuela prepared for "onslaught" of global economic crises, says Finance Minister, Venezuelanalysis.com, Aug 10. http://venezuelanalysis.com/news/6417

Appendix 2
Important Meetings Held by World Leaders to Address the 2008 Global Financial Crisis

Date	Place	Participants
June 18–19, 2012	Los Cabos, Mexico	G20
June 17, 2012	Los Cabos, Mexico	G7 finance ministers
March 1–2, 2012	Brussels	European Council
January 30, 2012	Brussels	Informal meeting of members of the European Council
December 8–9, 2011	Brussels	European Council
November 12–13, 2011	Honolulu, USA	19th APEC Economic Leaders' Meeting
November 3–4, 2011	Cannes, France	G20
October 23, 2011	Brussels	European Council
September 10, 2011	Marseille	G8 Deauville Partnership finance ministers
September 9–10, 2011	Marseille	G7 finance ministers and central bank governors
July 21, 2011	Brussels	Meeting of heads of state or government of the Euro area
June 23–24, 2011	Brussels	European Council
March 24–25, 2011	Brussels	European Council
March 17, 2011	Japan	G7 finance ministers telephone conference
March 11, 2011	Brussels	extraordinary European Council
February 4, 2011	Brussels	European Council
December 16–17, 2010	Brussels	European Council
November 21, 2010	Ireland	G7 finance ministers
November 13–14, 2010	Yokohama, Japan	18th APEC Economic Leaders' Meeting
November 11–12, 2010	Seoul, Korea	G20
October 28–29, 2010	Brussels	European Council
October 8, 2010	Washington DC	G7 finance ministers and central bank governors
September 16, 2010	Brussels	European Council
June 26–27, 2010	Toronto, Canada	G20
June 17, 2010	Brussels	European Council
March 25–26, 2010	Brussels	European Council

(continued)

C. Y.-Y. Lin et al., *National Intellectual Capital and the Financial Crisis in Argentina, Brazil, Chile, Colombia, Mexico, and Venezuela*, SpringerBriefs in Economics,
DOI: 10.1007/978-1-4614-8921-4, © The Author(s) 2014

(continued)

Date	Place	Participants
February 11, 2010	Brussels	Informal meeting of heads of state or government of the European Union
February 5–6, 2010	Iqaluit, Nunavut, Canada	G7 finance ministers and central bank governors
December 10–11, 2009	Brussels	European Council
November 19, 2009	Brussels	Informal meeting of heads of state or government of the European Union
November 14–15, 2009	Singapore	17th APEC Economic Leaders' Meeting
October 29–30, 2009	Brussels	European Council
October 3, 2009	Istanbul, Turkey	G7 finance ministers and central bank governors
September 24–25, 2009	Pittsburgh, USA	G20
September 17, 2009	Brussels	Informal meeting of heads of state or government of the European Union
June 18–19, 2009	Brussels	European Council
June 12–13, 2009	Lecce, Italy	G8 finance ministers
April 24, 2009	Washington DC	G7 finance ministers and central bank governors
April 2, 2009	G20 London Summit, United Kingdom	G20
March 19–20, 2009	Brussels	European Council
February 2009	Rome	G7 finance ministers and central bank governors
December 11–12, 2008	Brussels	European Council
November 2008	Peru	G20 APEC
November 22–23, 2008	Lima, Peru	16th APEC Economic Leaders' Meeting
November 14–15, 2008	Washington D.C., USA	G7
October 15–16, 2008	Brussels	European Council
October 10, 2008	Washington, DC	G7 Finance Ministers
September 1, 2008	Brussels	Extraordinary European Council
July 7–9, 2008	Tokyo, Japan	34th G8 Summit
June 19–20, 2008	Brussels	European Council
June 13–14, 2008	Osaka	G8 Finance Ministers Meeting
March 13–14, 2008	Brussels	European Council
February 9, 2008	Tokyo	G7 Finance Ministers and Central Bank Governors Meeting

For further information
http://g20mexico.org/en/g20/previous-leaders-summits
http://www.g8.utoronto.ca/finance/index.htm
http://video.consilium.europa.eu/ecofin/
http://www.european-council.europa.eu/council-meetings/conclusions
http://www.apec.org/

Appendix 3
Indicators in Each Type of Capital

Human capital index	*Market capital index*
1. Skilled labor*	1. Corporate tax*
2. Employee training*	2. Cross-border venture*
3. Literacy rate	3. Openness of culture*
4. Higher education enrollment	4. Globalization*
5. Pupil-teacher ratio	5. Transparency*
6. Internet subscribers	6. Image of country*
7. Public expenditure on education	7. Exports of goods
Process capital index	*Renewal capital index*
1. Business competition environment*	1. Business R&D spending
2. Government efficiency*	2. Basic research*
3. Intellectual property rights protection*	3. R&D spending/GDP
4. Capital availability*	4. R&D researchers
5. Computers in use per capita	5. Cooperation between universities and enterprises*
6. Convenience of establishing new firms*	6. Scientific articles
7. Mobile phone subscribers	7. Patents per capita (USPTO + EPO)

Remarks
1. Financial capital is the logarithm of GDP per capita adjusted by purchasing power parity
2. Indicators marked with an asterisk (*) are rated qualitatively using a scale of 1–10
3. Indicators with objective numbers are transformed to 1–10 scores, by calculating the ratio to the highest number in that indicator and then multiply 10
4. Readers can refer to the book National Intellectual Capital: A Comparison of 40 Countries for model validation details (www.nic40.org)

C. Y.-Y. Lin et al., *National Intellectual Capital and the Financial Crisis in Argentina, Brazil, Chile, Colombia, Mexico, and Venezuela*, SpringerBriefs in Economics,
DOI: 10.1007/978-1-4614-8921-4, © The Author(s) 2014

Appendix 4
Definition of the 29 Indicators

Indicators	Definition
Human capital	
Skilled labor*	Whether skilled labor is readily available
Employee training*	Whether employee training is a high propriety in companies
Literacy rate	Adult (over 15 years) literacy rate as a percentage of population
Higher education enrollment	Percentage of population that has attained at least tertiary education
Pupil-teacher ratio	Ratio of teaching staff to students
Internet subscribers	Number of internet users per 1,000 people
Public expenditure on education	Total public expenditure on education (percentage of GDP)
Market capital	
Corporate tax encouragement*	Whether corporate taxes encourage entrepreneurial activity
Cross-border venture*	Whether international transactions can be freely negotiated with foreign partners
Openness to foreign culture*	Whether the national culture is open to foreign culture ideas
Attitudes toward globalization*	Whether attitudes toward globalization are generally positive in a given society
Transparency*	Whether transparency of government policy is satisfactory
Country image*	Whether the image abroad of a given country encourages business development
Exports of goods	Exports of goods (Percentage of GDP)
Process capital	
Business competition environment*	Whether competition legislation is efficient in preventing unfair competition
Government efficiency*	Whether government bureaucracy hinders business activity
Intellectual property rights protection*	Whether intellectual property rights are adequately enforced

(continued)

C. Y.-Y. Lin et al., *National Intellectual Capital and the Financial Crisis in Argentina, Brazil, Chile, Colombia, Mexico, and Venezuela*, SpringerBriefs in Economics,
DOI: 10.1007/978-1-4614-8921-4,

(continued)

Indicators	Definition
Capital availability*	Whether cost of capital encourages business development
Computers in use per capita	Number of computers per 1,000 people
Convenience of establishing new firms*	Whether creation of firms is supported by legislation
Mobile phone subscribers	Number of subscribers per 1,000 inhabitants
Renewal capital	
Business R&D spending	Business expenditure on R&D (per capita)
Basic research*	Whether basic research enhances long-term economic development
R&D spending/GDP	Total expenditure on R&D (percentage of GDP)
R&D researchers	Total R&D personnel nationwide per capita (Full-time work equivalent per 1,000 people)
Cooperation between universities and enterprises*	Whether knowledge transfer is highly developed between universities and companies
Scientific articles	Scientific articles published by origin of author (per capita)
Patents per capita (USPTO + EPO)	USPTO and EPO total patents granted (per capita)
Financial capital	
GDP per capita (PPP) (From IMF)	Gross domestic product based on purchasing-power-parity (PPP) per capita

Appendix 5
48 Countries by Cluster and by Continent

This booklet series covers a total of 48 countries in 11 country clusters. China, Brazil and South Africa are grouped twice to maintain cluster completeness. China is in both Greater China region and BRICKS region, Brazil is in both BRICKS region and Latin American region, and South Africa is in both BRICKS region and in Cluster 5.

Eleven country clusters:

1. Portugal, Italy, Greece, Spain
2. Greater China region (China, Hong Kong, Singapore, Taiwan)
3. Brazil, Russia, India, China, Korea, South Africa (BRICKS)
4. Indonesia, Malaysia, the Philippines, Thailand
5. Israel, Jordan, Turkey, South Africa
6. Bulgaria, Czech Republic, Hungary, Romania, Poland
7. Austria, Belgium, the Netherlands, Switzerland
8. France, Germany, Ireland, United Kingdom
9. Argentina, Brazil, Chile, Colombia, Mexico, Venezuela
10. Australia, Canada, Japan, New Zealand, USA
11. Denmark, Finland, Iceland, Norway, Sweden

48 countries by continent:

Europe—24 countries

Nordic Europe—Denmark, Finland, Iceland, Norway, and Sweden

Western Europe—Austria, Belgium, France, Germany, Ireland, Netherlands, Switzerland, and UK

Southern Europe—Greece, Italy, Portugal, and Spain

Eastern Europe—Russia

East Central Europe—Bulgaria, Czech Republic, Hungary, Poland, Romania, Turkey

Americas—8 countries

North America—Canada, USA

Latin America—Argentina, Brazil, Chile, Colombia, Mexico, Venezuela

Australia—2 countries

Australia and New Zealand

C. Y.-Y. Lin et al., *National Intellectual Capital and the Financial Crisis in Argentina, Brazil, Chile, Colombia, Mexico, and Venezuela*, SpringerBriefs in Economics,
DOI: 10.1007/978-1-4614-8921-4,

Asia—13 countries

East Asia—China, Hong Kong, Japan, Korea, and Taiwan

West Asia—Israel, Jordan

Southeast Asia—Indonesia, Malaysia, Philippines, Singapore, and Thailand

South Asia—India

Africa—1 country

South Africa

Appendix 6
National Intellectual Capital Scores and Ranking for 48 Countries (2005–2010)

C. Y.-Y. Lin et al., *National Intellectual Capital and the Financial Crisis in Argentina, Brazil, Chile, Colombia, Mexico, and Venezuela*, SpringerBriefs in Economics,
DOI: 10.1007/978-1-4614-8921-4,

2005–2010	Human capital		Market capital		Process capital		Renewal capital		Financial capital		Overall IC	
Mean	6.420		5.409		5.345		3.658		9.115		29.946	
SD	1.217		1.085		1.454		2.056		0.690		5.840	
Country	Score	Ranking	Score	Ranking	Score	Ranking	Score	Ranking	Score	Ranking	Score	Ranking
Argentina	5.370	36	3.340	47	3.038	47	1.413	45	8.755	34	21.916	45
Australia	7.205	15	6.199	12	6.938	9	4.927	16	9.695	11	34.964	13
Austria	7.229	14	6.203	11	6.982	8	5.296	12	9.708	10	35.418	11
Belgium	7.666	8	5.519	23	5.924	21	4.706	17	9.635	14	33.450	19
Brazil	4.757	44	4.589	38	3.076	46	1.753	36	8.481	40	22.656	42
Bulgaria	5.493	34	4.929	31	4.054	36	1.589	41	8.646	37	24.710	35
Canada	7.855	6	6.137	13	6.464	15	5.064	14	9.710	9	35.229	12
Chile	5.414	35	6.663	5	5.163	28	1.710	37	8.784	32	27.734	30
China	4.942	39	5.184	28	3.746	40	2.099	33	7.967	44	23.938	40
Colombia	4.941	40	4.677	36	3.951	37	1.435	44	8.348	42	23.352	41
Czech Republic	5.995	30	5.720	18	5.378	25	2.905	24	9.271	27	29.269	25
Denmark	8.545	1	6.662	6	7.642	1	6.587	6	9.665	13	39.101	3
Finland	7.601	9	6.232	10	7.399	3	7.755	3	9.606	17	38.593	4
France	6.956	20	4.141	45	5.730	22	4.500	20	9.585	18	30.912	23
Germany	6.761	23	5.630	19	6.489	14	5.796	9	9.612	16	34.287	17
Greece	5.986	31	4.216	43	4.113	35	2.168	32	9.440	23	25.923	31
Hong Kong	6.564	25	8.090	2	7.209	5	3.277	23	9.794	4	34.934	14
Hungary	6.674	24	4.836	32	5.095	29	2.301	29	9.046	29	27.952	29
Iceland	8.357	3	5.614	21	6.561	12	5.931	8	9.713	8	36.154	8
India	3.926	48	5.620	20	3.556	42	1.954	34	7.285	48	22.340	44
Indonesia	4.062	47	4.832	33	3.257	44	1.519	42	7.594	46	21.263	47
Ireland	7.145	16	6.816	3	6.711	11	4.101	21	9.768	5	34.541	16
Israel	8.040	4	5.954	16	6.454	17	7.091	4	9.414	24	36.953	6

(continued)

(continued)

2005–2010	Human capital		Market capital		Process capital		Renewal capital		Financial capital		Overall IC	
Mean	6.420		5.409		5.345		3.658		9.115		29.946	
SD	1.217		1.085		1.454		2.056		0.690		5.840	
Country	Score	Ranking	Score	Ranking	Score	Ranking	Score	Ranking	Score	Ranking	Score	Ranking
Italy	6.471	28	4.155	44	5.184	27	2.745	26	9.479	22	28.035	28
Japan	7.581	10	4.820	34	6.209	18	6.473	7	9.576	19	34.659	15
Jordan	5.345	37	5.341	26	4.411	32	2.212	30	7.865	45	25.174	33
Korea	6.964	19	5.123	29	5.282	26	4.595	19	9.383	25	31.348	22
Malaysia	6.538	26	6.410	9	5.567	23	2.186	31	8.740	35	29.442	24
Mexico	4.871	42	4.491	39	3.226	45	1.237	48	8.781	33	22.606	43
Netherlands	7.312	12	6.761	4	6.879	10	5.163	13	9.739	7	35.855	10
New Zealand	7.123	18	5.999	15	6.460	16	3.701	22	9.380	26	32.662	21
Norway	7.936	5	6.055	14	7.008	7	4.961	15	9.987	1	35.947	9
Philippines	4.772	43	4.464	40	3.317	43	1.268	47	7.481	47	21.302	46
Poland	6.393	29	4.246	41	3.895	38	1.819	35	8.945	30	25.299	32
Portugal	6.882	22	4.801	35	5.470	24	2.467	27	9.224	28	28.844	26
Romania	5.829	32	4.219	42	3.806	39	1.685	38	8.594	39	24.133	39
Russia	5.530	33	3.860	46	3.588	41	2.349	28	8.822	31	24.150	38
Singapore	7.144	17	8.306	1	7.506	2	5.416	11	9.961	2	38.334	5
South Africa	4.708	45	4.976	30	4.472	31	1.677	39	8.472	41	24.306	37
Spain	6.524	27	4.649	37	5.033	30	2.787	25	9.484	21	28.476	27
Sweden	8.385	2	6.563	7	7.174	6	7.780	2	9.673	12	39.575	1
Switzerland	7.575	11	6.481	8	7.374	4	7.988	1	9.753	6	39.172	2
Taiwan	7.244	13	5.823	17	6.026	20	5.425	10	9.526	20	34.044	18
Thailand	5.310	38	5.524	22	4.365	33	1.436	43	8.304	43	24.938	34

(continued)

(continued)

2005–2010	Human capital		Market capital		Process capital		Renewal capital		Financial capital		Overall IC	
Mean	6.420		5.409		5.345		3.658		9.115		29.946	
SD	1.217		1.085		1.454		2.056		0.690		5.840	
Country	Score	Ranking	Score	Ranking	Score	Ranking	Score	Ranking	Score	Ranking	Score	Ranking
Turkey	4.703	46	5.227	27	4.167	34	1.666	40	8.690	36	24.453	36
United Kingdom	6.939	21	5.440	24	6.090	19	4.697	18	9.626	15	32.793	20
USA	7.695	7	5.348	25	6.558	13	6.715	5	9.886	3	36.202	7
Venezuela	4.884	41	2.761	48	2.545	48	1.277	46	8.625	38	20.092	48

Appendix 7
Country Profile: Additional Statistics

1. International Reserves in Millions of US$

Country	2005	2006	2007	2008	2009	2010
Argentina	19,587	20,525	35,651	48,806	44,931	45,498
Brazil	61,498	59,196	108,817	194,223	189,398	242,561
Chile	15,365	15,940	15,323	17,844	23,267	25,585
Colombia	12,642	14,963	18,847	21,928	23,271	24,896
Mexico	64,054	75,949	75,773	91,042	85,471	101,313
Venezuela	19,928	24,934	23,909	20,250	17,555	15,276

Source: Global Finance http://www.gfmag.com/

2. GDP per capita—PPP Current international dollar

Country	2005	2006	2007	2008	2009	2010
Argentina	10,860	12,045	13,339	14,413	14,524	15,854
Brazil	8,603	9,166	9,900	10,528	10,453	11,239
Chile	12,237	13,064	13,919	14,604	14,289	15,002
Colombia	7,340	7,990	8,688	9,085	9,192	9,566
Mexico	12,482	13,435	14,154	14,557	13,681	14,430
Venezuela	9,992	11,113	12,130	12,733	12,184	11,829

Source: World Economic Outlook Database http://www.imf.org/external/ns/cs.aspx?id=28

3. GDP (PPP)—share of world total_%

Country	2005	2006	2007	2008	2009	2010
Argentina	0.74	0.76	0.79	0.82	0.83	0.87
Brazil	2.80	2.76	2.78	2.85	2.86	2.93
Chile	0.35	0.35	0.35	0.35	0.35	0.35
Colombia	0.56	0.56	0.57	0.58	0.59	0.59
Mexico	2.29	2.29	2.24	2.21	2.10	2.10
Venezuela	0.47	0.49	0.50	0.52	0.50	0.47

Source: World Economic Outlook Database http://www.imf.org/external/ns/cs.aspx?id=28

C. Y.-Y. Lin et al., *National Intellectual Capital and the Financial Crisis in Argentina, Brazil, Chile, Colombia, Mexico, and Venezuela*, SpringerBriefs in Economics,
DOI: 10.1007/978-1-4614-8921-4, © The Author(s) 2014

4. Gross domestic expenditure on R&D as a % of GDP

Country	2005	2006	2007	2008	2009	2010
Argentina	0.44	0.46	0.49	0.51	0.51	0.51
Brazil	0.93	0.83	1.02	1.1	1.09	1.23
Chile	0.65	0.68	0.68	0.68	0.68	0.67
Colombia	0.17	0.17	–	0.16	0.15	0.15
Mexico	0.39	0.43	0.5	0.46	0.37	0.37
Venezuela	0.46	0.29	0.25	0.23	0.23	2.39

Source: IMD World Competitiveness Yearbook 2006–2011

Glossary

ANEFE the National Agreement for Family Economy and Employment

Basel II Basel II is the second of the Basel Accords, which are recommendations on banking laws and regulations issued by the Basel Committee on Banking Supervision. Basel II, initially published in June 2004, was intended to create an international standard for banking regulators to control how much capital banks need to put aside to guard against the types of financial and operational risks banks face

CEI Centro de Economia Internacional

CIA The USA Central Intelligence Agency

CPB CPB Netherlands Bureau for Economic Policy Analysis (CPB) was founded in 1945. Research at CPB is carried out on CPB's own initiative, or at the request of the government, parliament, individual members of parliament, national trade unions or employers federations

CPS Country Partnership Strategy

CPI Consumer price inflation

ECLAC Economic Commission for Latin America and the Caribbean

EFTA The European Free Trade Association

EIA environmental impact assessment

EU European Union

FDI Foreign direct investment

GCI GCI Global Competitiveness Index (published by World Economic Forum)

GDP Gross domestic product

GDP per capita (ppp) Gross domestic product per capita adjusted by purchasing power parity

GHG greenhouse gas

C. Y.-Y. Lin et al., *National Intellectual Capital and the Financial Crisis in Argentina, Brazil, Chile, Colombia, Mexico, and Venezuela*, SpringerBriefs in Economics,
DOI: 10.1007/978-1-4614-8921-4,

IDB Inter-American Development Bank

ILO International Labor Office

IMD International Institute for Management Development

IMF International Monetary Fund

HC Human capital

Long-term NIC Long-term oriented national intellectual capital, represented by human capital and renewal capital

MC Market capital

MNE Multi-national enterprise

MILA the Mercado Integrado Latinoamericano

NIC National intellectual capital

OECD Organization for Economic Cooperation and Development

PC Process capital

ppp Purchasing power parity

RCI Rural Capitalization Incentive

R&D Research and development

RC Renewal capital

SECO Swiss Economic Development Cooperation

SD Standard Deviation

SDC Swiss Agency for Development and Cooperation

Short-term NIC Short-term oriented national intellectual capital, represented by market capital and process capital

SMEs Small and Medium-Sized Enterprises

Three time periods For the convenience of comparing ranking changes, the six years data were separated into three time periods, namely 2005–2006, 2007–2008, and 2009–2010. Two years each represents "before, during, and after" the 2008 global financial crisis. Even though Euro zone is still in sovereign debt trouble as of mid-2012, the time partition is based on the financial crisis progression in the epicenter. The signs of financial trouble appeared in 2007 and the crisis was declared over in the third quarter of 2009

USPTO United States Patent and Trademark Office

VAT Value-added tax

References

Alsema A (2009) Colombian deficit sets limits on further stimulus, Dec 23. Colombia Reports. http://colombiareports.com/colombia-news/economy/7454-colombian-deficit-sets-limits-on-further-stimulus-minister.html

Altman RC (2009) The great crash, 2008: a geopolitical setback for the west. Foreign Affair, the Council on Foreign Relations, Jan 2. http://www.foreignaffairs.com/articles/63714/roger-c-altman/the-great-crash-2008

Anees A (2010) Venezuelan economy in 2010—the bad hair day. Global Financial Crisis, May 3. http://www.arifanees.com/global-financial-crises/venezuelan-economy-in-2010-the-bad-hair-day.html

Arguello R (2009) The international economic crisis, the trade channel, and the Colombian economy. Perfil de Coyuntura Economica 13:9–32. http://aprendeenlinea.udea.edu.co/revistas/index.php/coyuntura/article/viewFile/3295/3059

Barnes S (2010) Resolving and avoiding unsustainable imbalances. In: OECD Economic Surveys: Euro Area 2010. http://www.keepeek.com/Digital-Asset-Management/oecd/economics/oecd-economic-surveys-euro-area-2010/resolving-and-avoiding-unsustainable-imbalances_eco_surveys-euz-2010-5-en

Barton D, Krell A (2011) Managing crises and shaping the future of Chile: an interview with Sebastian Pinera. McKinsey Q. https://www.mckinseyquarterly.com/Public_Sector/Management/Managing_crises_and_shaping_the_future_of_Chile_An_interview_with_Sebastian_Pinera_2841

Bermudez I (2009) Argentina responds to crisis with unorthodox measures. Forum of Federations. http://www.forumfed.org/en/products/magazine/vol8_num2/argentina-unorth-measures.php

Bleger L (2011) Latin American in better conditions to face the global crisis: financial regulations in Argentina, Brazil, Chile, Colombia, Mexico and Peru, research project "Financial instability and financial regulation in Latin America" supported by Ford Foundation. http://www.itf.org.ar/pdf/documentos/83-2011.pdf

Bloomberg Business Week (2010) Mexico, Brazil start trade negotiations. Bloomberg Business week, Nov 8. http://www.businessweek.com/ap/financialnews/D9JCAK1G0.htm

Briones I (2010) Chile country report. In: Bertelsmann Stiftung (ed) Managing the crisis: a comparative assessment of economic governance in 14 economies. Bertelsmann Stiftung, Gütersloh, 2010. http://www.bertelsmann-transformation-index.de/pdf/Chile.pdf

Brown C (2009) Argentina's economic challenges. The Dialogue, Feb 12. http://www.thedialogue.org/page.cfm?pageID=32&pubID=1819

Cadena A, Remes J, Restrepo A (2011) Fulfilling the promise of Latin America's cities. Mckinsey Q. https://www.mckinseyquarterly.com/Economic_Studies/Country_Reports/Fulfilling_the_promise_of_Latin_Americas_cities_2845

Cárdenas M (2008) Global financial crisis: Is Brazil a bystander? http://www.brookings.edu/opinions/2008/1015_financial_crisis_cardenas.aspx

C. Y.-Y. Lin et al., *National Intellectual Capital and the Financial Crisis in Argentina, Brazil, Chile, Colombia, Mexico, and Venezuela*, SpringerBriefs in Economics, DOI: 10.1007/978-1-4614-8921-4,

Central Intelligence Agency (CIA) (2012) The world factbook, U.S.A. Central Intelligence Agency. https://www.cia.gov/library/publications/the-world-factbook/geos/ch.html
Centro de Economia Internacional (CEI) (2009) Argentine economic review No. 59. CEI Government Argentina. http://www.cei.gov.ar/userfiles/pea59eng.pdf
Coutino A, Fuentes JP, Leon MD (2012) Latin America Outlook 2013: recovering the potential. Moody's Analytics, Dec 11. http://www.economy.com/dismal/article_free.asp?cid=236121
CPB Netherlands Bureau for Economic Policy Analysis (2012) Macro economic outlook (MEV) 2013, Sept 18. http://www.cpb.nl/en/publication/macro-economic-outlook-2013
Dahlman C (2009) Different innovation strategies, different results: Brazil, Russia, India, China and Korea. In: Chandra V, Erocal D, Padoan PC, Braga CP (eds) Innovation and growth: Chasing a moving frontier. OECD and International Bank for Reconstruction and Development/The World Bank
Del Pont M (2011) Argentine economy expanded 9.2% in 2010 and begins 2011 with a 6% floor. Merco Press South Atlantic News Agency, March 19. http://en.mercopress.com/2011/03/19/argentine-economy-expanded-9.2-in-2010-and-begins-2011-with-a-6-floor
Doerig HU (2009) In a better position than before the crisis: The Swiss financial market has 'AAA' opportunities for the future, Credit Suisse Group, Sept 11. https://www.credit-suisse.com/news/doc/speech_doerig_nzz_en.pdf
ECLAC, Economic Commission for Latin America and the Caribbean—United Nations (2009) Preliminary overview of the economies of Latin America and the Caribbean. http://www.eclac.org/publicaciones/xml/3/38063/Brazil.pdf
Economy Watch (2010) Colombia economic structure. Economy Watch, March 15. http://www.economywatch.com/world_economy/colombia/structure-of-economy.html
Edvinsson L, Malone MS (1997) Intellectual capital: realizing your company's true value by finding its hidden brainpower. HarperBusiness, New York
Elliott L (2012) UK economic recovery will be slow, OECD warns. The Guardian, Nov 27. http://www.guardian.co.uk/business/2012/nov/27/uk-economic-recovery-slow-oecd
England J (2011) Is Argentina's economy overheating? The Argentina Independent, Aug 10. http://www.argentinaindependent.com/currentaffairs/newsfromargentina/is-argentinas-economy-overheating/
European Commission (2012) The EU economy: sailing through rough waters. European Commission News, Nov 7. http://ec.europa.eu/news/economy/121107_en.htm
Fackler M (2008) Financial crisis spreads to emerging nations. The New York Times, Oct 23. http://www.nytimes.com/2008/10/24/business/worldbusiness/24won.html
Faga F (2008) The U.S. financial crisis affects Latin America: The Colombian context. Council on Hemispheric Affairs. http://www.coha.org/the-us-financial-crisis-affects-latin-america-the-colombian-context/
Garces A (2011) Colobmia's outward FDI jumps. Latin Business Chronicle. http://www.latinbusinesschronicle.com/app/article.aspx?id=5166
Global Finance (2012a) Argentina country report. Global Finance online data. http://www.gfmag.com/gdp-data-country-reports/328-argentina-gdp-country-report.html#axzz2PfcepgKP
Global Finance (2012b) Chile country report. Global Finance online data. http://www.gfmag.com/gdp-data-country-reports/300-chile-gdp-country-report.html#axzz1yexyZJyT
Gregorio J (2008) The Chilean economy in the current global financial crisis. Central Bank of Chile. http://www.bcentral.cl/politicas/presentaciones/consejeros/pdf/2008/jdg18112008.pdf
Gupta G (2011) Oil fails to lubricate Venezuelan economy. Minyanville Business News, Feb 24. http://www.minyanville.com/businessmarkets/articles/venezuela-news-venezuela-economy-libya-news/2/24/2011/id/32988
Gurria A (2009) Recent reforms strengthening Brazil's resilience to economic crisis, July 14. http://www.oecd.org/document/44/0,3746,fr_21571361_44315115_43294124_1_1_1_1,00.html
Gutierrez H (2011) Latin American economic outlook 2011: Fiscal policy and the social contract, OECD Development Centre. http://www.oecd.org/dataoecd/36/58/47578097.pdf

Heritage Foundation (2012a) Economic freedom—Argentina. http://www.heritage.org
Heritage Foundation (2012b) Economic freedom—Chile. http://www.heritage.org
Heritage Foundation (2012c) Economic freedom—Colombia. http://www.heritage.org
Heritage Foundation (2012d) Economic freedom—Mexico. http://www.heritage.org
Heritage Foundation (2012e) Economic freedom—Venezuela. http://www.heritage.org
Hutchinson M (April 2, 2009) Chile positioned well for the financial crisis. Nuwire Investor. http://www.nuwireinvestor.com/articles/chile-positioned-well-for-the-financial-crisis-52785.aspx
International Labor Office (ILO) (2010a) G20 country briefs—Argentina. G20 meeting of Labor and Employment Ministers. http://www.dol.gov/ilab/media/events/G20_ministersmeeting/G20-Argentina-brief.pdf
International Labor Office (ILO) (2010b) G20 country briefs: Brazil's response to the crisis. G20 Meeting of labor and employment ministers, 20–21 April 2010
International Labor Office (ILO) (2010c) G20 country briefs—Mexico's response to the crisis. G20 meeting of Labor and Employment Ministers. http://www.dol.gov/ilab/media/events/G20_ministersmeeting/G20-Mexico-brief.pdf
International Monetary Fund (IMF) (2013) World economic outlook update: gradual upturn in global growth during 2013, Jan 23. http://www.imf.org/external/pubs/ft/weo/2013/update/01/
Kehoe T (2010) The current financial crisis in Spain: what should we learn from the great depressions of the twentieth century? University of Minnesota and Federal Reserve Bank of Minneapolis, 18th Barcelona Lecture, Barcelona G.S.E. and Banc Sabadell, Feb 2010
Larsen P (2009) Economic crisis and imperialist attaches pose new challenge for the revolution, Sept 10. http://www.marxist.com/venezuela-economic-crisis-imperialist-attacks.htm
Levy-Yeyati E, Cohan L (2011) Latin America economic perspectives: innocent bystanders in a brave new world. Latin America Initiative at Brookings, Nov 2011. http://www.brookings.edu/~/media/research/files/reports/2011/11/economic%20perspectives/11_economic_perspectives.pdf
Lin CYY (2011) Leveraging intellectual capital for future competitiveness in Finland. Presentation at Tekes, Helsinki, 10 Nov 2011
Lin CYY, Edvinsson L (2011) National Intellectual Capital: a comparison of 40 countries. Springer Publishing Co., New York
Lopez L, Cascione S (2011) Brazil economy surges in 2010: growth seen cooling. Reuters, March 3. http://www.reuters.com/article/2011/03/03/us-brazil-economy-idUSTRE7222QZ20110303
Melconian C (2011) The Argentine economy is "a time-bomb ticking" warns economist. Merco Press South Atlantic News Agency, Oct 25. http://en.mercopress.com/2011/10/25/the-argentine-economy-is-a-time-bomb-ticking-warns-economist
Mendonça JR (2010) The impact of the international financial crisis on Brazil. http://www.realinstitutoelcano.org/wps/portal/rielcano_eng/Content?WCM_GLOBAL_CONTEXT=/elcano/elcano_in/zonas_in/international+economy/ari38-2010
Michener G (2011) Brazil's economic outlook a mixed bag. Latin America Monitor, July 28. http://www.csmonitor.com/World/Americas/Latin-America-Monitor/2011/0728/Brazil-s-economic-outlook-a-mixed-bag
Ministry of Finance and Public Credit (2009) Colombia and economic crisis. Ministry of Finance and Public Credit Republic of Colombia. http://www.irc.gov.co/portal/page/portal/MinHacienda/elministerio/prensa/Historicos/2009/BID/Brochure%20MinHacienda%20ENG.pdf
Morales M, Matthews J (2011) Argentina's economy and risks. Reuters Buenos Aires, March 28. http://www.reuters.com/article/2011/03/28/us-latam-summit-argentina-idUSTRE72R1XD20110328
Morgan J (n.d.) Venezuela to aid key sectors in stimulus package. Latin American Herald Tribune. http://www.laht.com/article.asp?CategoryId=10717&ArticleId=342500
Nanto DK (2009) The global financial crisis: analysis and policy implications. CRS report for Congress RL34742, Congressional Research Service, Oct 2. http://www.fas.org/sgp/crs/misc/RL34742.pdf

Norris F (2011) Crisis is over, but where's the fix? The New York Times, March 10. http://www.nytimes.com/2011/03/11/business/economy/11norris.html?pagewanted=1
OECD (2011) Economic survey of Mexico 2011, OECD. http://www.oecd.org/document/34/0,3746,en_2649_33733_47781730_1_1_1_1,00.html
OECD (2012a) Chile—Economic forecast summary (May 2012), OECD. http://www.oecd.org/document/61/0,3746,en_2649_34109_45274749_1_1_1_1,00.html
OECD (2012b) Mexico—Economic forecast summary (May 2012), OECD. http://www.oecd.org/document/26/0,3746,en_2649_34109_45270042_1_1_1_1,00.html
OECD and UN (2012) Latin American economic outlook 2012: transforming the state for development, Development Centre of OECD and United Nations Economic Commission for Latin America and the Caribbean (ECLAC). http://www.oecd.org/dataoecd/38/35/48965859.pdf
Porzecanski AC (2009) Latin America: the missing financial crisis. United Nations ECLAC Office in Washington, Oct 2009. http://www.eclac.org/washington/publicaciones/xml/8/37908/Porzecanski_final_draft_LC.WAS.L.104_SEP09_PREPRINT_rev_3.pdf
Pradhan M (2012) 2012: Split down the middle. Morgan Stanley, Jan13. http://www.morganstanley.com/views/gef/
Reavis C (2009) The global financial crisis of 2008–2009: the role of greed, fear and oligarchs. MIT Sloan Management Case #09-093, published 22 July 2009
Reinhart CM, Rogoff KS (2009) This time is different: eight centuries of financial folly. Princeton University Press, Princeton, ISBN: 9780691142166
Reinoso AF (2010) Peru and Colombia: Similar strategies, contrasting reactions. Latin American Trade Network, Aug 2010. http://www.latn.org.ar/web/wp-content/uploads/2011/03/FLA_GTA_06_Peru-Col_Sept06.pdf
Rodriguez M (2011) Democracy in hard times: Venezuela. Americas Barometer Insights: 2011 Number 69, Vanderbilt University. http://www.vanderbilt.edu/lapop/insights/IO869en.pdf
Saatdjian M (2008) How and why Venezuela will weather the financial crisis, Vevenuelanalysis.com, Oct 10. http://venezuelanalysis.com/analysis/3863
Sanchez M (2010) Mexico's economic outlook: challenges and opportunities. Deputy Governor of the Bank of Mexico presented at the conference "Latin American 2010: Economic, business and trade forecast", Center for Hemispheric Policy, University of Miami, Feb 5. http://www.banxico.org.mx/publicaciones-y-discursos/discursos-y-presentaciones/discursos/%7B90A0BE2B-F2C3-0118-02A5-2EDDA1894287%7D.pdf
Schwab K (ed) (2011) The global competitiveness report 2011–2012. World Economic Forum, Geneva
Segura B (2011) Argentine economy forecasted to expand 8% in 2011 with inflation ranging 25%. Merco Press South Atlantic News Agency, April 16. http://en.mercopress.com/2011/04/16/argentine-economy-forecasted-to-expand-8-in-2011-with-inflation-ranging-25
Sidaoui J, Ramos-Francia M, Cuadra G (2010) The global financial crisis and policy response in Mexico. In: The Global crisis and financial intermediation in emerging market economies. Bank for International Settlements, BIS Papers chapters, number 54-17. www.bis.org/publ/bppdf/bispap54q.pdf
Sullivan MP (2011) Venezuela: Issues for congress. Congress Research Service, CRS report for congress, R40938, March 11. http://www.hsdl.org/?view&did=7621
Swiss Economic Development Cooperation (SECO) (2009) Colombia: Country strategy 2009–2012, Federal Department of Economic Affairs FDEA, State Secretariat for Economic Affairs SECO. www.seco-cooperation.admin.ch/laender/02004/index.html
TDS, Travel Document Systems (2012) Brazil economy, Jan 8. http://www.traveldocs.com/br/economy.htm
The Economist (2011) Venezuela's economy: oil leak. The Economist, Feb 24. http://www.economist.com/node/18233412
The New York Times (2012) Argentina. The New York Times, April 19. http://topics.nytimes.com/top/news/international/countriesandterritories/argentina/index.html

US State Department (2011) Background note: Chile. US State Department, Diplomacy in Action, Dec 16. http://www.state.gov/r/pa/ei/bgn/1981.htm

Valadao M, Porto NG (2009) Brazilian response to international financial crisis, May 21. http://studentorgs.law.smu.edu/getattachment/International-Law-Review-Association/Resources/LBRA-Archive/15-3/SMB308.pdf.aspx

Vera Azaf L (2010) The Venezuelan economy after the global economic crisis. Monthly Economic Bulletin, Mercantil Banco Universal, Economic Research Unit, March 2010. http://www.bancomercantil.com/mercprod/site/tools/info_economica/reportes/ing/mensual/monthly_economic_bulletin_march2010.pdf

Villarreal MA (2010) The Mexican economy after the global financial crisis. Congressional Research Service 7-5700, Sept 16. www.fas.org/sgp/crs/row/R41402.pdf

Weisbrot M (2010a) Venezuela is not Greece. The Guardian. http://www.guardian.co.uk/commentisfree/cifamerica/2010/may/06/venezuela-greece-economic-crisis

Weisbrot M (2010b) Venezuela's recovery depends on economic policy. Center for Economic and Policy Research, April 2010. http://www.cepr.net/index.php/op-eds-&-columns/op-eds-&-columns/venezuelas-recovery-depends-on-economic-policy

Weisbrot M, Ray R, Sandoval L (2009) The Chavez administration at 10 years: the economy and social indicators. Center for Economic and Policy Research. http://www.cepr.net/documents/publications/venezuela-2009-02.pdf

Woods R (2010) Chile's economy is 'back on track,' set for 5% growth this year, IMF says, Bloomberg, Sept 29. http://www.bloomberg.com/news/2010-09-29/chile-s-economy-is-back-on-track-set-for-5-growth-this-year-imf-says.html

Xinhua (2009) Colombian economy grapples with global financial crisis. Xinhua People's Daily Online, July 7. http://english.people.com.cn/90001/90778/90858/90863/6694918.html

Author Index

C. Y.-Y. Lin et al., *National Intellectual Capital and the Financial Crisis in Argentina, Brazil, Chile, Colombia, Mexico, and Venezuela*, SpringerBriefs in Economics,
DOI: 10.1007/978-1-4614-8921-4, © The Author(s) 2014

Subject Index

C. Y.-Y. Lin et al., *National Intellectual Capital and the Financial Crisis in Argentina, Brazil, Chile, Colombia, Mexico, and Venezuela*, SpringerBriefs in Economics,
DOI: 10.1007/978-1-4614-8921-4,

MIX
Papier aus verantwortungsvollen Quellen
Paper from responsible sources
FSC® C105338

If you have any concerns about our products,
you can contact us on
ProductSafety@springernature.com

In case Publisher is established outside the EU,
the EU authorized representative is:
Springer Nature Customer Service Center GmbH
Europaplatz 3, 69115 Heidelberg, Germany

Printed by Libri Plureos GmbH
in Hamburg, Germany